"In a world where teens are too often viewed as incapable of earnest discipleship practices, Lindsey Carlson's book communicates a refreshing and much-needed message: maturity starts now. *Growing in Godliness* offers basic concepts, accessible tools, and practical steps for teens to understand themselves as devoted followers of Christ. And it offers parents a rare gift as well: the golden opportunity of faith-infused dialogue with their young-adult child."

Jen Wilkin, Director of Classes and Curriculum, The Village Church; author, *Women of the Word*; *None Like Him*; and *In His Image*

"So much of the person we turn out to be hinges on decisions made in our teenage years. Those years can be filled with wonder, but also with fears and dangers. In this book, Lindsey Carlson gives a practical guide for how young women can use their teenage years to grow in Christ. This advice could be life-changing for you, or for someone you love."

Russell D. Moore, President, The Ethics & Religious Liberty Commission of the Southern Baptist Convention

"*Growing in Godliness* is hands down my favorite book for teen girls. Its fresh writing, theological grit, accessible advice, grace-driven counsel, and practical application of the means of grace make me want to put it in the hands of all of the girls I know. No Pollyanna fluff or theological bricks here. I started to read this in the hospital, watching my own teenage girl recover from major surgery, and the sections that I read filled me with hope in the dark hours of my daughter's pain."

Rosaria Butterfield, Former Professor of English, Syracuse University; author, *The Gospel Comes with a House Key*

"As children grow into teenagers, there is also a growing sense of urgency in their parents. There's so much to say, so much to teach, and still so much to learn. It's hard to know where to start. Parents can trust that *Growing in Godliness* will give their teen girls a great place to start in their discipleship. This practical resource is grounded in the gospel and candidly conversational to reach teen girls where they are."

Gloria Furman, author, *Missional Motherhood*

"It's not easy to be a teen girl. The world tells you to follow your heart, your peers encourage you to conform to their image, and even your own emotions threaten to overwhelm you. Which of us didn't long for a trustworthy friend to guide us through those messy middle school years? Thankfully Lindsey Carlson is that friend—warm, wise, funny, and direct—pointing teens to the only source of certainty and hope in a confusing world. Again and again, she brings girls back to God and his word, encouraging teens to shake off the worldliness that stunts their spiritual growth and to reach instead for Christ alone. As a pastor's wife and mother, I couldn't be more pleased to have this book on my shelf. Give it to the teens in your church or, better yet, gather a group and read it together. *Growing in Godliness* is an invaluable resource for young teen girls and the adults who care about their souls."

Megan Hill, author, *Praying Together* and *Contentment*; Editor, The Gospel Coalition

"While I have no experience in being a teenage girl, I've got a fair bit of experience in raising them. And from the perspective of a father, I can say this book represents exactly the kind of knowledge and wisdom that will serve them well for the few years they are teenagers and for the lifetime beyond."

Tim Challies, blogger, Challies.com

"*Growing in Godliness* is one of the best resources I've read on the topic of discipleship in the teen years. Lindsey Carlson is relatable, engaging, understanding, wise, and laugh-out-loud funny as she helps teen girls grasp their need for God and learn how to grow in faith. I plan to read this book with my daughter and will be recommending it for all her friends!"

Melissa Kruger, Director of Women's Content, The Gospel Coalition; author, *In All Things: A Nine-Week Devotional Bible Study on Unshakeable Joy*

"As a fellow victim of the glamour shots trend of the 1990s, I can relate to Lindsey Carlson's described desire for quick fixes and microwaved maturity. But she has given teenage girls a gift in these pages—not only a description of what it means to be spiritually mature but also a relatable guide for pursuing that growth. I'm thankful my own daughter will have these words to encourage her as she grows in grace."

Catherine Parks, author, *Real and Empowered: How God Shaped 11 Women's Lives (and Can Shape Yours Too)*

"This book was a heart-changing read. It altered my perspective on many things. The author had lots of stories, which made reading it fun. Now I can't wait to grow in godliness!"

Emily H., age 11

GROWING IN GODLINESS

Lindsey Carlson

GROWING
IN
GODLINESS

A Teen Girl's Guide to
Maturing in Christ

WHEATON, ILLINOIS

Library of Congress Cataloging-in-Publication Data

Names: Carlson, Lindsey, 1982– author.
Title: Growing in Godliness : a teen girl's guide to maturing in Christ / Lindsey Carlson.
Description: Wheaton, Illinois : Crossway, [2019] | Includes bibliographical references and index. | Audience: Ages 12–19.
Identifiers: LCCN 2018046531 (print) | LCCN 2018054103 (ebook) | ISBN 9781433563850 (pdf) | ISBN 9781433563867 (mobi) | ISBN 9781433563874 (epub) | ISBN 9781433563843 (tp) | ISBN 9781433563874 (ePub)
Subjects: LCSH: Teenage girls—Religious life. | Christian teenagers—Religious life.
Classification: LCC BV4551.3 (ebook) | LCC BV4551.3 .C374 2019 (print) | DDC 248.8/33—dc23
LC record available at https://lccn.loc.gov/2018046531

Crossway is a publishing ministry of Good News Publishers.

BP		29	28	27	26	25	24	23	22	21	20	19
15	14	13	12	11	10	9	8	7	6	5	4	3	2	1

For my daughter,
Madeline Claire Carlson—
may you grow in the grace and knowledge
of our Lord and Savior Jesus Christ
all of your days.

With hope and love,
Mama

Contents

Introduction

Congratulations.

If you are reading this book, you've finally hit the teen years, or you're about to. Gone are the days of parent-planned playdates; you're firing off texts to your friends faster than your mom can find her phone. You're negotiating privileges like wearing makeup, staying home alone, and babysitting the neighbor's kids for a little extra cash. You're growing up.

You can expect your teen years to be filled with all kinds of growth. First, you're growing physically. Just ask your poor parents, whose pantry shelves are always empty. I'm sure they've noticed the way your jeans always seem too short and your shoes too small. It's like one night you went to bed as a kid and the next morning your body decided to wake up as a grown-up.

Of course, also present are the less-than-enjoyable growing and often raging hormone levels. Cue the unwelcome unpredictability of acne and surging emotions. So long, steadiness; hello, stereotypical mood swings. Growing up means learning to woman-handle your body's hormonal rises and falls and learning to deal with the happy-one-minute-and-weeping-the-next feelings that come along with them.

You're growing socially, too. Don't worry, so are all of your friends. You're each learning to evaluate the kind of friends you want around and the kind of friend you want to be. Sometimes this means outgrowing certain friendships and gaining new ones. Combine this social switcheroo with your influx of growing hormones and emotions, and it makes the teenage years a tad bit challenging.

Unfortunately, there's no rest for the weary teen. You're still growing as a student, and schoolwork doesn't ease up as you try to make sense of all your new physical, emotional, and social growth spurts!

As a teenager, you are surrounded by growth potential. At school, in your relationships, when dealing with your emotions, and in your changing physical body, growth is a good thing. Ask the doctor checking your height and weight each year. Ask the teacher recording your homework and test grades to ensure your successful progress. Ask your parents who love and guide you and pray you'll grow into a mature adult. Growth is a sign of life, and the resulting fruit that blossoms is a sign of maturity.

Now I'd like to ask you something. Are you also *growing in godliness*? Because this area of growth and maturity is more important than all the rest. Beloved, as a Christian you are called to grow in godliness until you are conformed to the image of Jesus (Rom. 8:29). You do this by growing in the grace and knowledge of Jesus Christ (2 Pet. 3:18). Christian growth should take top priority in your life not only as a teenager, but as long as you're alive. In the following chapters, we will examine what the Christian's growth in godliness looks like and learn to strive for maturity in Christ.

As a teenager longing to follow Jesus, you are on the front end of what should be a lifelong pursuit of spiritual growth! I pray your desire to read this book is an indication of your desire to look more like Jesus. Even though you're young and busy growing in so many ways, in Christ you have all it takes to grow in godliness.

So, strive for growth:

> Until we all attain to the unity of the faith and of the knowl-
> edge of the Son of God, to mature [wo]manhood, to the mea-
> sure of the stature of the fullness of Christ, so that we may no
> longer be children, tossed to and fro by the waves and carried
> about by every wind of doctrine, by human cunning, by crafti-
> ness in deceitful schemes. Rather, speaking the truth in love,
> we are to *grow up in every way* into him who is the head, into
> Christ, from whom the whole body, joined and held together
> by every joint with which it is equipped, when each part is
> working properly, makes the body grow so that it builds itself
> up in love. (Eph. 4:13–16)

Your maturity in Christ is meaningful and necessary both for
you personally and for the building up of the body of Christ. Your
growth is imperative. God wants to use every area of your life—
each experience, challenge, and privilege—as spiritual fertilizer,
feeding your growth in godliness.

How does God intend for you to grow in godliness? That's what
this book is all about. In the following chapters I'll challenge you to
live to grow in Christ, to find purpose in all you do, and to trust God's
sovereign goodness. We'll talk about your limitations, and I'll point
you to the tools God uses to equip you through his Word, his church,
and prayer. I'll show you why it's important to keep a close watch
on your words, emotions, and spiritual fruit, as they are all signs of
spiritual life and health. There's a lot to learn, but it's all within reach.

Congratulations. You've picked up the book, you've made it
through the intro, and now you're ready to go. "Now to him who
is able to strengthen [and grow] you according to my gospel and
the preaching of Jesus Christ . . . to bring about the obedience of
faith—to the only wise God be glory forevermore through Jesus
Christ!" (Rom. 16:25–27). Let's get growing!

Part 1

PARTNER WITH GOD

1

Live to Grow

As a child, I was always in a hurry to grow up. I wanted the privileges and freedom that came with maturity, but I didn't want to wait through the awkward period of growing. It was this desire for unearned maturity that prompted me to ask for a makeover for my eleventh birthday. It was 1993, and a company called Glamour Shots was happy to prey upon my desire for change. For a fee, I could walk inside the local mall, and the Glamour Shots professionals promised to change my look, making me glamorously grown-up.

Right down the hall from the wafting smells of pizza and corn dogs in the mall's food court, my hair was teased, curled, and hair sprayed until it stood up by itself. My face was painted with layers of thickly caked stage makeup, my eyes sparkled with glittery eye shadow, and red lipstick only highlighted the fact that my crooked teeth were in desperate need of orthodontia. They dressed me up in feather boas and leather jackets bedazzled with rhinestones.

The makeover culminated in a photo session where I was coached to pose in laughably unrealistic ways: tossing my head back, staring solemnly into the camera, or placing my fist under my chin. After a few hours and a sizable financial investment on my parents' part, I walked out with pictures that made me look like a forty-year-old real estate agent. Happy birthday to me.

My "before and after" transformation was bizarre. They had contoured my cheekbones and jawline, dressed me like an adult, and dramatically backlit my photos, and in the end, I sure did look different. But, *creepy* different. I didn't look more mature. I looked like a little girl whose dress-up play had gone terribly wrong. When I left the mall that day, I went home and washed all the hairspray and makeup off and returned to my regularly scheduled life as a normal makeup-less eleven-year-old. Growing up required more than makeup, big hair, and a bedazzled jacket.

Sometimes as Christians, we can become so preoccupied with looking mature that we attempt to skip the process of actually growing up. Like little children wearing their mom's high heels, we clip-clop around pretending to be all grown up before we've had the chance to gain the wisdom necessary to become mature. In order to avoid the Glamour Shots edition of Christian growth, we need God's help to grasp the beauty of true growth in godliness.

The Original Picture

I love a good "before and after" reveal. I can't wait to see how beautiful my teenage daughter's once-crooked teeth will look after her braces come off. And I am guilty of fast-forwarding through hour-long episodes of television shows like *Fixer Upper* just to catch the big reveal of the beautiful house at the end. As a growing Christian, you are likely painfully aware of all your imperfections and the ways you need to grow in holiness and your ability to honor God. You know where you need God to work. But before the work begins on your *before* picture, you'll need to understand the *original* picture.

Most *before* pictures aren't complete pictures; they leave important pieces out. When my daughter's orthodontist took *before* pictures of her crooked adult teeth for her medical chart, she ignored her original set of perfectly straight baby teeth. She cared only about the unruly progression of the adult teeth. As Chip and Joanna Gaines escort homebuyers and cameras through dilapidated homes on *Fixer Upper*, I always wonder what the homes originally looked like when they were first built. How impressive were they before the previous owners ruined them? As viewers, we never see the glorious *original* picture that preceded the less-than-glorious *before* picture. Instead, we cut in on the dirty middle. The place in need of assistance. The work in progress.

Your *original* picture dates back to before you were born, when God spoke the heavens and earth, planets and stars, seas, mountains, plants, and animals into being and called humanity *very good* (Gen. 1:31). He formed you *imago Dei*, in the image of God. By nature, you are wonderful because you were made to reflect God throughout creation, bringing him glory in all you do. In the original picture, your spiritual parents Adam and Eve stood smiling in the garden, still in good standing with God. They trusted him, enjoyed fellowship with him, and walked in obedience.

Like the dilapidated house ruined by previous owners, your original glorious picture eroded before you stepped foot on the scene. You wouldn't have done any better. In Genesis 3, Adam and Eve listened to the voice of the enemy, questioned God's goodness, disobeyed his command, and ate the forbidden fruit, and the eyes of both were opened. The Lord said to the woman, "What is this that you have done?" and in righteous anger cursed the man and woman for their disobedience. So long, life of ease and peace with God. Hello, painful labor against ground now filled with thorns, sweat-filled brows, and eventual death. You have never had the chance to enjoy the original picture.

The Before Picture

Your life picks up right where most transformations begin—in the middle of the *before* picture—broken and rebellious. While you were originally created by God to wonderfully reflect his image, instead you rebelled like Eve. Ephesians 2:1–3 explains "*you* were dead in the trespasses and sins in which you once walked, following the course of this world" and "were by nature children of wrath, like the rest of mankind." You are stained by the curse of sin and an enemy of God. Without God's intervention, you are decaying and headed for destruction.

There is an answer to your brokenness. Ephesians 2:4–7 goes on to say, "*But God*, being rich in mercy . . . *even when we were dead* in our trespasses, made us *alive together with Christ*—by grace you have been saved—and raised us up with him and seated us with him in the heavenly places in Christ Jesus, so that in the coming ages he might show the immeasurable riches of his grace in kindness toward us in Christ Jesus." Your broken *before* picture has been granted the hope of redemption. God rebuilds what sin destroyed by making you alive in Christ and then renovating your brokenness until you look even more beautiful.

The After Picture

We love the part where the old is gone and the new has come because we instinctively know the *after* picture is always better than the *before* picture. For the Christian, completion waits for us in heaven. "Behold, the dwelling place of God is with man. He will dwell with them, and they will be his people, and God himself will be with them as their God. He will wipe away every tear from their eyes, and death shall be no more, neither shall there be mourning, nor crying, nor pain anymore, for the former [broken] things have passed away" (Rev. 21:3–4). God is making all things new (21:5) and will reveal his work in the *after* picture upon completion saying, "It is done! I am the Alpha and the Omega, the beginning and the end" (21:6).

While we love what's revealed in the *after* picture, we don't love to wait. It's why I attempted to find maturity at Glamour Shots and why I always fast-forward Chip and Joanna. But before any big reveal, there is always a lot of behind-the-scenes work to produce real change. The rebuilder must identify what stays and what goes, remaking inside and outside until all shines like new. As Christ works in the hearts of his people, he cleanses and prepares them to present to his Father "without spot or wrinkle or any such thing, that she might be holy and without blemish" (Eph. 5:27). Stripping away the brokenness until you are "altogether beautiful" with "no flaw in you" (Song 4:7) takes work.

Work in Progress

As Christians, we are works in progress, awaiting full redemption. Stained by sin, we are no longer the original picture we were created to be. Made alive in Christ, we are no longer dead in our sin, decaying like the dilapidated *before* versions of our selves. But we aren't yet the fully redeemed *after* picture either. We are in the work-in-progress stage of being made new.

We want our love to "abound more and more, with knowledge and all discernment, so that [we] may approve what is excellent, and so be pure and blameless for the day of Christ" (Phil. 1:9–10). We strive to become "blameless and innocent, children of God without blemish in the midst of a crooked and twisted generation" (Phil. 2:15), not for our own glory but for the glory of God. But right now, Christ is at work, establishing our hearts "blameless in holiness" before God at his coming (1 Thess. 3:13). Until then, we must "grow in the grace and knowledge of our Lord and Savior Jesus Christ" (2 Pet. 3:18) until the work is complete.

Growing in Godliness

From the instant God makes you alive in him, he begins working in your heart through the power of the Holy Spirit, in a process called *sanctification*. Sanctification is an all-day, everyday process that makes you more and more free from sin and more and more like Christ in your actual life.[1] This process cleans the "yuck" of sin in your heart and makes you more godly. Godliness simply means more God-likeness. If you are a Christian, you are growing in godliness as you wait for God to complete his *after* picture. You have a role to play in your sanctification. While your role is not equal in ability or power, God uses your willing cooperation and submission as part of the collaborative process. Philippians 2:12–13 specifies you are to work out your salvation with fear and trembling, while also assuring you it is indeed God who is at work within you both to will and to work for his good pleasure. God is pleased to work in your life as you trust and submit to him. When you partner with God by surrendering to Christ, you have the ability to become increasingly holy and righteous, *like God*. This growth in godliness, or God's-likeness, grants you an increasing capacity to exalt God. Author Jerry Bridges describes *godliness* as the "devotion to God which results in a life that is pleasing to him."[2] Bridges also writes:

> The practice of godliness is an exercise or discipline that focuses upon God. From this Godward attitude arises the

character and conduct that we usually think of as godliness. So often we try to develop Christian character and conduct without taking the time to develop God-centered devotion. We try to please God without taking the time to walk with him and develop a relationship with him. This is impossible to do.[3]

You can't fake or rush Christian maturity. There is no Glamour Shots version of holiness that is convincing to God on the day of redemption; only the work of the Spirit will do. In order to know God and please him, you must work with God to *grow in godliness*. Surrender to the work of the Holy Spirit and ask him to give you wisdom to understand the character of God and the desire to be more like him.

The Big Reveal

If you are alive in Christ, your spiritual growth is facilitated by the inexhaustible resources of the Holy Spirit. As you await the big reveal, trust that you are in good and powerful hands. Second Peter 1:3–4 assures believers:

> His divine power has granted to us all things that pertain to life and godliness, through the knowledge of him who called us to his own glory and excellence, by which he has granted to us his precious and very great promises, so that through them you may become partakers of the divine nature, having escaped from the corruption that is in the world because of sinful desire.

Can you even imagine what it will be like to no longer experience the corruption of sin and to finally find freedom from your sinful desires? What a gift it is to know that one day you will enjoy *all* of God's precious promises! When God reveals the glorious *after* picture of his bride made new, the change will be drastic, and in response you will worship *him* (Rev. 22:3). Until that day:

> Make every effort to supplement your faith with virtue, and virtue with knowledge, and knowledge with self-control, and self-control with steadfastness, and steadfastness with god-liness, and godliness with brotherly affection, and brotherly affection with love. For if these qualities are yours and *are increasing*, they keep you from being ineffective or unfruitful in the knowledge of our Lord Jesus Christ. (2 Pet. 1:5–8)

Live to grow in godliness. Partner with God in the pursuit of ho-liness until Christ returns for the big reveal, and we will all see the glorious *after* picture together. Until that day, get to work as a work in progress, striving to see God's glory revealed in increasing measure in your life.

Grow Up by Progressing in Godliness

The mature Christian woman continually submits herself to the pursuit of holiness.

Practice Progressing in Godliness

* *Ask* yourself if you identify more with the "dead in sin" or the "alive together with Christ" description found in Ephesians 2. If you are a Christian, what are some examples of growth in godliness that you've observed in your life?

* *Identify* a few ways that your life has been a representation of "dead in sin," and if you're growing in godliness, a few ways that you'd like to see God's power at work.

* *Write* 2 Peter 1:3 on a note card and tape it to your mirror or your school binder. Work to commit this promise to memory.

* *Pray* for God to give you patience as you work to grow in godliness. Ask him to help you rely on his power at work in your life. Pray that he would soften your heart and reveal areas of weakness or brokenness that need your attention.

2

Get to Work

When my daughter Madeline was little, I made the mistake of implying she might someday grow up to be a mommy. A look of offense swept over her face, her hands migrated angrily to her hips, and she stomped in protest, underscoring her strong opposition: "Mama! I'm not going to be a *mommy*! I'm going to be a *cowgirl*!" Crystal-clear career ambitions for a five-year-old.

The clarity dated back to her second birthday when my aunt gifted her with a small plastic horse. "Eduardo" set the course of Madeline's affections for years to come. He rarely strayed from her squishy toddler grasp, and over the years she insisted we add countless other horsey friends to her collection. Her father and I must have purchased every version of plastic horse sold on the shelves of our local Target. Madeline knew each one by name.

Madeline played almost exclusively with horses, talked almost exclusively about horses, and shared her knowledge about horses with anyone who would listen. She knew random trivia about their breeds, their life expectancies, and how to care for them. She wore horse-themed clothing, slept with a mountain of horse stuffed animals on her bed, and read every horse book she could get her hands on. Birthdays and Christmas were all opportunities to accumulate more horse-related gifts. In Madeline's young little heart—Horses. Were. Life. Nothing could distract her from pursuing all her horsey dreams.

As a child, Madeline's sense of purpose guided her decisions. Because she loved horses, she spent her time playing with horses and spent her money buying anything and everything horse-related. Have you ever loved something as much as Madeline loved horses? Is there an area of your life that you pursue with as much passion and purpose?

Maybe you want to be a professional singer, athlete, or artist. Do you spend your time learning, studying, and practicing in order to become whatever it is you've set your hopes on? Now, think of your interest in growing in godliness. Do you give your time, attention, and focus to the pursuit of knowing more about God? Or does the pursuit of growing in godliness feel like an imposition to your plans?

What Is Your Purpose?

Love fuels devotion. If you love soccer and feel like your life's purpose is to become a professional soccer player, you will pursue growing as a soccer player with everything you have. As you grow in your love for the Lord, you should notice a growing desire to devote yourself to fulfilling *his* purposes for your life.

Proverbs 16:4 says, "The LORD has made everything for its purpose." Your life has a purpose grander than any hobby or career ambition. Do you know what this purpose is? As a Christian growing in godliness, you must learn to identify this purpose in order to pursue it. Will God tell you his plan, or is it up to you to figure it out on your own?

Your life's purpose as a Christian is not mysterious or hidden like buried treasure. And by the end of this chapter I hope you'll find that a God-centric sense of purpose will help guide all your choices, giving you wisdom for how you spend your time, energy, and money, for the rest of your life. Let's begin by establishing a basic working definition of *purpose*.

Purpose is the reason you exist and the primary goal of your life.

What Is God's Purpose for Your Life?

God created you with one specific and overarching purpose for your life. It is the clear and concrete reason you exist and the primary goal for your life. It isn't unique or different from any other Christian's purpose. God doesn't intend for you to figure out your purpose all on your own. You are not living in some cruel obstacle course that you must stumble blindly through. Your purpose isn't mysterious.

You can figure it out today. Your ability to successfully fulfill your purpose in life doesn't depend on your skills, abilities, resources (or lack thereof), or your ever-changing passions. It can't be thrown offtrack by a bad grade in algebra, or by failing to enroll in an activity or training program, by an injury on the field, or by moving to another school. God reveals his purpose for your life in his Word so that you can successfully learn, plan, and prepare, and grow with confidence!

When God created Adam and Eve in his image, he placed them in the garden of Eden to work and keep it, and gave them dominion over all the earth (Gen. 1:26; 2:15), Scripture tells us he did so for his glory (Isa. 43:7). He formed us for himself, that we might declare his praise (Isa. 43:21)! As followers of Christ we are part of "a chosen race, a royal priesthood, a holy nation, a people for his own possession, [called to] proclaim the excellencies of him who called [us] out of darkness into his marvelous light" (1 Pet. 2:9). The Lord created all of humanity, including you, in his image for *his purposes*. King David writes in 1 Chronicles 16:29–31: "Ascribe to the LORD the glory due his name; bring an offering and come before him! Worship the LORD in the splendor of holiness; tremble before him, all the earth; yes, the world is established; it shall never be moved. Let the heavens be glad, and let the earth rejoice, and let them say among the nations, 'The LORD reigns!'"

God's purpose for your life is to bring him glory in all you do.

Why Glorify His Name?

If this is the first time you've considered God's desire for his own glory, you might think this sounds selfish. If you demanded all of your friends and family spend their lives bringing you praise, honor, and adoration, *you* would be selfish because you are not worthy. Sorry. If God were like you, your concern would be valid. But God is different from you, and gloriously so.

God is supremely unique and good. He is God, and there is none like him. He created life, breath, and everything else. He spoke the heavens and earth into existence. He commands the winds and moves the mountains. He puts kings into power and brings them down. He alone is holy and righteous and has the authority to judge us all. He is also slow to anger and abounding in steadfast love and faithfulness. He sent his own Son to redeem us. He guides, directs, equips, and sanctifies through his Spirit. And one day, when he conquers the power of darkness and tramples Satan underfoot, he will rule the universe in uncontested power and authority. Not only is God not selfish to purpose us for his infinite praise, but he also is right to do so because he alone is worthy.

We are told that one day all the inhabitants of heaven will cry out before the throne of God, "Worthy are you, our Lord and God, to receive glory and honor and power, for you created all things, and by your will they existed and were created" (Rev. 4:11).

Even though God alone is worthy of your worship and you have been purposed to praise him, you probably don't find yourself naturally giving him all the honor he is due. This is because your natural instincts are stained by sin and tend to lead you to gather praise for yourself instead. But God patiently endures with you, "in order to make known the riches of his glory" for his children, who are "vessels of mercy, which he has prepared beforehand for glory" (Rom. 9:23). Your life is filled with God's mercy in order that he might use you to make his name known and display his glory.

The apostle Paul writes to the Corinthian church, "You are not your own, for you were bought with a price" (1 Cor. 6:19–20). As you learned in the first chapter of this book, the mature Christian woman continually submits herself to the pursuit of holiness. In order to grow in godliness, you must live with God's purpose in mind. You are called to "glorify God in your body" (1 Cor. 6:20), doing *all things* to the glory of God (1 Cor. 10:31). God wants more than your Sunday mornings. He wants your life. He wants to change your desires, your talents, and your pursuits—all for his glory. God wants your life to be one of worship. Worship is your purpose as a believer growing in godliness and your purpose in God's *after* picture when you're made complete in Christ.

Purpose vs. Work

Now it's time to discuss the way you work out your purpose. We defined *purpose* as the reason you exist and the primary goal of your life. Now let's define *work*.

Work is the means by which you fulfill your purpose.

Today, you are a student. If your purpose as a student is to get an education, then going to classes, taking notes, completing homework, and taking tests are all part of the work required to fulfill your purpose as a student. Learning is your work. Because God's purpose for your life is to bring him glory in all you do, your work is anything that accomplishes the task of bringing him glory. This means that you don't have to work as a professional missionary or a Sunday school teacher to bring God glory; you could glorify God as a musician or a math teacher. No matter what your future holds, you are called to be faithful to God in your work today as a Christian growing in godliness.

Your work is where you live out your purpose as a Christ-follower. This means you could work for the glory of God as a mom, a cowgirl, a missionary, or endless other imaginable callings. Jesus did the work of a carpenter by trade, but woodworking wasn't his passion and purpose in life. As he preached in the synagogues in Judea, he clarified his actual purpose: "I must preach the good news of the kingdom of God . . . for I was sent *for this purpose*" (Luke 4:43). When he stood before Pilate and was questioned, "So you are a king?" Jesus answered, "You say that I am a king. For this *purpose* I was born and for this *purpose* I have come into the world—to bear witness to the truth. Everyone who is of the truth listens to my voice" (John 18:3–7). Jesus's purpose was to glorify God and do his work.

Your work should look like Jesus's work. No, not carpentry. Your work should be to do the work of your Father. Growing in godliness entails working mindfully toward the mission of bringing God glory.

Get to Work on Purpose

If you've made the decision to follow Jesus with your life, then you've committed your life to one grand purpose: bringing God glory. Fan the flames of your love for God by investing your time, efforts, and energy in learning everything you can about him. Grow in godliness by worshiping him with your life. How do you fuel your love and devotion to God? Do you spend your time in ways that encourage you to become more like Jesus? Do you pray for the Holy Spirit to help you shine like a light in the world? Strive to love God and serve God with focused, unswerving passion and tenacity, worshiping God with all your life.

Worship God in eighth grade art class as you sharpen your sketching skills. Bring him glory at the lunch table as you share the gospel with a friend. Glorify him while you diligently make your way through algebra with a humble heart and by modeling the fruit of the Spirit to your friends and teachers. God will use your work to serve as the hands and feet of Christ and as his witness to the world when you pursue him. All work—schoolwork, housework, jobs outside the home, creating, writing, inventing, and even playing—is an opportunity for worship. Live on purpose by striving to bring God glory in each job and responsibility you take on.

What is your passion? What would your friends or your parents say your purpose in life is? How can you use your skills, hobbies, and passions to grow in godliness and pursue your purpose as a lifelong worshiper? You are not too young to begin asking and answering these questions. Get to work on purpose by glorifying God with your life today.

Grow Up by Working to Worship

The mature Christian woman purposes to bring God glory with her life and her work.

Practice Working to Worship

* *Ask* God to help you identify ways your life could bring him glory. Are there ways you could worship him with your time, talents, and treasures? How could you more purposefully serve the Lord as a student?

* *Identify* areas of your life where you excel. Are you ever tempted to worship your own name instead of his name? Identify ways you might be able to purposefully work to worship God. If you're not sure, ask your parents or a trusted mature Christian friend or leader.

* *Write* 1 Chronicles 16:24 on a note card and place it in a location where you're most often tempted to work for your own glory or worship yourself. If you're a piano prodigy, put it on the piano. If you excel as a student, perhaps put it in your school notebook. Wherever you decide to work for God's glory, use this Scripture as a reminder of the call to worship.

* *Pray* and ask the Lord to help you work diligently, with joy, for the sake of his kingdom. Ask him to help you grow in your understanding of worship, and be quick to recognize when you're glorifying yourself instead of him.

3

Relax and Trust Him

As the oldest child in my family, I had a reputation for being a tad bossy. My younger brother David bore the brunt of my bossiness. Most of our playtime memories hold to one common theme: *I am in charge.* When we played house, I played the mother and David was the child I corrected. When we played school, I was the teacher and he was the student following instructions. When we pretended we were on a television show, I was the host with the microphone and David was the one being interviewed. When we played restaurant, office, or around-the-world travelers . . . you get the picture. I was in charge.

My control-freak nature did not end with playtime. One summer afternoon my mom asked me to make my brother a peanut butter sandwich, and I wasn't in the mood. Instead of doing what my mom had asked, I sabotaged David's lunch by playing a little trick on him. On one side of the bread I spread peanut butter, on the other side butter, and in between, a nice thick layer of powdered parmesan cheese. After smashing the bread together, I cut it into neat triangles and casually passed it on to him.

In a disappointing turn of events, he praised my new concoction and spent the next few years asking me to recreate the delicacy. My parents were not as amused. They pleaded with me to be a good sister and to treat David kindly. Instead, I continued to scheme, fool, and use my sisterly sway to monopolize television viewing, seats in the car, chore divisions, and anything else I saw fit to selfishly manipulate for my own good and gain.

Years later, I'm still learning to put my bossy tendencies to death. In my flesh, I would love to have complete control over everyone and everything in my life. I'd love to be in charge of every detail from the weather, to my children's moods, to how my life will pan out ten years from now. Naively, I can be tempted to think that if I could control my circumstances, then I could avoid pain and heartache and manufacture perfect happiness. Can you relate? Do you try to be the boss of your own life? Are you tempted to think you know what you need, better than God?

How do you respond when God answers no to a prayer request, gives you something other than what you've asked for, or leads you through an unwelcome challenge or trial? Do you ever feel angry, fearful, or anxious when you don't know what the future holds? Do you worry God's forgotten you? Have you ever tried to take over for him or attempted to manipulate him into giving you what you want? In order to grow in Christian maturity, you must outgrow your power-grabbing tendencies and ask God to replace them with a confident understanding and trust of his power and authority in your life. God's plans for your life are not selfish; he's not like a conniving older sibling who cannot be trusted. He is not holding out on you. You don't need to wonder whether or not you should trust God's character and his love for you.

Growing in godliness means outgrowing your childish, unholy ways and learning that you are not the boss. God is in control, seated on his throne, ruling and reigning over everything from gray skies to good grades. So relax, and learn to trust him.

God Is Sovereign

Where your self-appointed sovereignty is unearned, unjust, and unkind, not to mention mostly imaginary, God's sovereignty is righteously deserved. He created the heavens (Isa. 45:18) and the earth (Jer. 33:2). He created and breathed life into all men and women and gave us dominion over all the earth. He established his throne, and his kingdom rules over all (Ps. 103:19), and in his hand are power and might so none can withstand him (2 Chron. 20:6). He alone rules supremely over the heavens, the earth, and everything in them. Your Father reigns forever, and his throne endures to all generations (Lam. 5:19). Because he created all, he rules over all. God is *sovereign*.

God is sovereign over the world at large, but he's also specifically sovereign over you. He knitted you together in your mother's womb (Ps. 139:13), determining details like your hair and eye color, the dimple in your chin, the size of your feet, your creativity, and your athleticism or lack thereof. He's sovereign over your home life, placing you in your family and ruling over your parents' jobs, finances, health, and ability to care for you. He's sovereign over your education, where and how you learn, allowing you to fail and pass tests, giving you encouraging teachers and difficult ones, and directing you as you explore new opportunities. He is sovereign over your social life—party invitations and cancelled plans, popularity and loneliness, even over bullies and peer pressure. Every area of your life is shaped by decisions made by the Lord (Prov. 16:33), and each experience passes through his hands because *all things* (Eph. 1:11) are subject to his authority.

God Is Good

In this broken world, *control* doesn't always imply inherent *goodness*. When I made my brother's sandwich, I had power over the peanut butter, but I didn't have the kindness of heart to use it for David's good. Spend any time in the Old Testament and you'll find plenty of examples of wicked kings who used their rule for evil purposes and were condemned by God as doing evil in the sight of the Lord. Mercy and goodness were not precursors when they abused authority. Because we so often see examples of power being misused, we tend to assume God might misuse power also. We believe we can't trust God's power over our lives because we can't trust people's authority and because we don't fully understand the character of God. But God's sovereignty is good news because God himself is good.

The psalmist says of God in Psalm 100:5: "The LORD is good; his steadfast love endures forever, and his faithfulness to all generations." God is majestic in holiness and awesome in glorious deeds (Ex. 15:11). He is a "refuge and strength, a very present help in trouble" (Ps. 46:1). He is a helper and an upholder of life (Ps. 54:4). He is "gracious and merciful, slow to anger and abounding in steadfast love" (Neh. 9:17). Just as the Lord led Israel with an everlasting love and continued his faithfulness (Jer. 31:3), he leads his children now with the same cords of kindness and bands of love (Hos. 11:4). Great is the Lord and greatly to be praised. God's power and mercy do not stand in opposition; instead they work together.

Jesus points out that God alone is *good* (Mark 10:18). He "cannot be tempted with evil" (James 1:13), so his plans and purposes for your life cannot be characterized by malicious intent. Instead, his plans are filled with goodness and mercy. Your motives are good sometimes, but his motives are 100 percent good and can always be trusted. God has demonstrated his goodness toward humanity from the very beginning; he created you even though he knew you'd stumble into sin. Instead of punishing you and casting you off forever, which would have been completely in his power, in his goodness he provided a plan of rescue through Christ and made a way for you to be redeemed and for you to be reconciled to God. Titus 3:4–5 says, "But when the *goodness* and *loving kindness* of God our Savior appeared, he saved us, not because of works done by us in righteousness, but according to *his own mercy*." Through the substitutionary death of Christ in your place, God shows off both his sovereign power to save you and his goodness in his willingness to do so.

In addition to the incredible gift of salvation, he's also responsible for providing you with every other blessing and gift you've been given. All of your good relationships, talents, abilities, material belongings, positive experiences, and successes are gifts from his hand because "every good gift and every perfect gift is from above, coming down from the Father of lights" (James 1:17). He equips you with "everything good that you may do his will," and he is "working in [you] that which is pleasing in his sight, through Jesus Christ, to whom be glory forever and ever" (Heb. 13:21). He has given you all that you have, and has placed you in your family, your school, your neighborhood, and your church at this time in history, for your good and his glory.

God Is Trustworthy

Why is understanding God's sovereignty and his goodness necessary for growing in godliness? Because you need tangible truths to point to when life gets hard and doubt looms large. God's proven track record of faithfulness reminds you he is trustworthy, even when you don't *feel* like he's working all things together for your good. When your plans get cancelled, or when you're left out, or your grades are failing, it would be easy to point the finger at God and ask, "Where were you, Lord?" When someone in your family faces cancer, divorce, or death, you may wonder, "Why'd you let this happen, God?" Is God in control and working even then?

It would be natural to assume that because God doesn't always give you what you want, he isn't loving. In the introduction I mentioned the call in Ephesians 4:13–15 to grow into Christian maturity so that you may "no longer be children, tossed to and fro by the waves" but instead to "grow up in every way" into Christ. One of the most common ways immature Christians are tossed by the waves of life is by their own failure to recognize God's sovereign goodness in the middle of their trials.

Author Jerry Bridges writes, "The sovereignty of God is often questioned because man does not understand what God is doing. Because he does not act as we think he should, we conclude he cannot act as we think he would."[1] An informed understanding of God's sovereignty and goodness will strengthen and equip you in the face of disappointment, hurt, and confusion when God's plans are different from yours. While *people* don't always act in your best interest, God always does, and sometimes he uses painful situations to conform you to Christlikeness.

God's sovereignty assures you that even when you don't understand his plans, you can trust him. Consider Job—his life is the ultimate portrait of suffering and personal loss. He was a blameless and upright man who feared God and turned away from evil (Job 1:1). But this didn't keep him from experiencing God's hand of sovereignty in the form of loss and heartache. When his servants died by sword and fire and his children were crushed to death when wind struck and collapsed their house, Job fell on the ground and worshiped (1:15–20). When God allowed Satan to strike Job with loathsome sores all over his body, Job refused to curse God. Instead, he responded, "Shall we receive good from God, and shall we not receive evil" (2:10)?

Job responds to suffering with spiritual maturity because the reality of God's sovereignty was paired with the comfort of a deeply rooted trust in God's good and loving character. In the midst of tragedy Job is not tossed by the waves but is able to confidently say, "As for me, I would seek God, and to God would I commit my cause, who does great things and unsearchable, marvelous things without number . . . [for] he wounds, but he binds up; he shatters, but his hands heal" (Job 5:8–9, 18). Job trusts that God is both in control and good. As chaos swirls in Job's life, he chooses to place his trust in God's ability to hold all things together.

Remember, your story is *in progress*; God is always working. When Joseph's brothers tossed him in a pit and left him for dead, it would have been easy for him to think his life was over. But in God's sovereign goodness, he used what was meant for evil for good (Gen. 50:20) and took Joseph from the pit to the palace in order to fulfill his plans for Joseph, his family, the Israelite people who would soon face famine, and the further unfolding of the kingdom of God. God's plans always take into account his plan for redemption. God remains seated sovereignly on his throne and ruling from heaven where he's triumphed over the mouths of lions, the belly of a fish, a fiery furnace, barren wombs, the edicts of kings, the chains of slavery, and ultimately the crucifixion of his Son. Nothing can stand against the plans of the Lord. Just as God had good plans for Job and Joseph, you can trust he has good plans for you.

Relax

God is in control. God is good. God is trustworthy. How can these truths help you grow in godliness? Knowing and believing that God is in control, good, and trustworthy helps you grow in godliness by convincing you that you are not the boss. God's sovereignty reminds you that you don't need to grasp for control of everything or get panicky when things don't go your way.

If you're a little bossy or a lot, there's hope for you. Grow in godliness and ask the Lord to mature your understanding of his sovereign goodness. You can change. Through the Holy Spirit's enabling, you can trust God and surrender your need for control. You've never really had it to begin with. Look at just a few of the ways God's sovereign goodness is already at work in your life today:

- *Showing you his truth*: "Now, O Lord God, you are God, and your words are true, and you have promised this good thing to your servant" (2 Sam. 7:28).
- *Giving you his Spirit to guide you*: "You gave your good Spirit to instruct them and did not withhold your manna from their mouth and gave them water for their thirst" (Neh. 9:20).
- *Pouring out mercy on you*: "The Lord is good to all, and his mercy is over all that he has made" (Ps. 145:9).
- *Sanctifying you (making you more like Jesus)*: "I am sure of this, that he who began a good work in you will bring it to completion at the day of Jesus Christ" (Phil. 1:6).
- *Giving you hope for the future*: "For I know the plans I have for you, declares the Lord, plans for welfare and not for evil, to give you a future and a hope" (Jer. 29:11).

So, relax. Trust God. He is sovereign over your life, and this is good news. God is not like a mean big sister. He's not sneaking parmesan cheese on your peanut butter. Your heavenly Father's care for you is sovereign, good, and trustworthy. Trust his rule because you trust his heart. You cannot escape God's good plans for your life because he fulfills his purposes. If God is for you, who can be against you? He who did not spare his own Son but gave him up for us all, how will he not also with him graciously give you all things (Rom. 8:31–32)?

Grow Up by Trusting God's Sovereign Goodness

The mature Christian woman finds comfort in trusting God's sovereignty over her life.

Practice Trusting God's Sovereign Goodness

* *Ask* God to reveal to you the ways you are tempted to grab control over your life. When are you the most disappointed to not get your way? How is the Holy Spirit convicting you to lay down the desire for control?
* *Identify* a time in your life when you didn't get your way, but God made it clear that his way was better. How did this help you to trust him more?
* *Write* Job 23:13–14 and list some examples of ways you're currently tempted to "turn" God back from doing what he desires for you.
* *Pray* for the Lord to give you the wise perspective of Proverbs 19:21: "Many are the plans in the mind of a man, but it is the purpose of the Lord that will stand." Confess your need for control and ask God to help you trust him with your plans and desires.

Part 2

DEPEND ON HIS WAYS

4

Learn from Your Limits

Over the course of sixteen television seasons, hundreds of thousands of undiscovered vocalists have looked to the reality television show *American Idol* in the hopes of launching their musical career. The new contestants flock to open auditions to sing before groups of talent scouts, then advance to a televised panel of judges, then move on to "Hollywood Week," all before the show turns the contestants over to the votes of the American people. The singers must prove to the judges that they are willing to learn from expert coaches, listen to advice, and grow in their singing abilities.

In Season 4, contestant number 14887 began her journey by pacing back and forth outside the audition room, wringing her hands. She whispered a prayer to calm her nerves and then took her place before the panel of judges. After a deep breath she began to sing. Melodically and effortlessly the notes floated through the air, but her interlaced fingers remained tensely anchored across her stomach. By the end, the judges were impressed by two things. Her voice. And her nerves.

Carrie Underwood had earned a ticket to Hollywood. But she'd need to work on her stage presence—learn to relax and sing through her nerves. As you know, Carrie listened to the critique and has continued to learn and grow. Not only did she earn Season 4's title of "American Idol," but she's the best-selling *American Idol* contestant of all time, now having won seven Grammy awards and sold more than 65 million records globally.

This is not how all *American Idol* auditions end. For every successful audition, hundreds more starry-eyed contestants have their dreams shattered before a watching world. Yet year after year, unqualified candidates file in to display their tone-deaf, pitchy, cracking, bizarrely unappealing voices to the masses. Perhaps no one has ever broken the bad news that singing isn't their strength. Personally, I think it's more likely that they haven't bothered to listen to criticism or the perspectives of those with wisdom to offer. When notable naysayer Simon Cowell says in his curt British accent, "I really believe you are the worst singer in the entire world," many of these arrogant contestants argue back: "I'm talented. I know I am. People tell me I can sing." Maybe they are talented, but they sure aren't humble or willing to grow and learn.

Proverbs 12:15 says, "The way of a fool is right in his own eyes, but a wise man listens to advice." When it comes to reality television, it's easy to laugh from the couch at the fool who clearly can't sing but argues as he's kicked to the curb. In real life, foolishness is neither funny nor desirable. In order to grow in godliness, you'll need humility and God's help to navigate your limitations with wisdom.

What Are Limits and Why Don't You Love Them?

Limitations, by definition, are *restrictions*; they will follow you through your teen years and into adulthood. Your alarm clock limits the amount of sleep you get each morning. Your pantry offers a limited supply of breakfast items. After breakfast you have a limited amount of time to put your dishes in the sink before your mom reminds you. You are limited, and in many ways you are used to limits. You are familiar enough with your humanity to understand you'll never grow up to be a unicorn and you can't shapeshift, time hop, or disappear into thin air. You have the same basic set of human limitations. You require air, food, and water to live, and so you breathe, eat, and drink without ever questioning God or his goodness for giving you limitations.

Certain limits you *do* mind. And in your teen years there seems to be an endless supply. Perhaps your parents limit your screen time, regulate how late you can stay up, and prevent you from eating twelve Twinkies for breakfast. At school your teacher might place limits on who you can sit with at lunch, how much you can talk or text during class, and how many days you have to make up late work. When you're with your friends, you might feel a limited ability to fit in because of your embarrassing flip phone or the fact that you don't gossip or watch the same kinds of movies. Or your growing body might suddenly limit you from fitting into your favorite pair of shoes from last spring or from having clear skin and good hair on school picture day. I'm sure you'd love to have the final say in overriding certain limits. Limits cramp your style.

While you're not likely to smile and say thank you to the adults in your life as they place limits on everything from the apps on your phone to the amount of apple pie you can eat, you likely know these boundaries are for your protection and good. Then why don't you love limitations and see them as a privilege and delight? Because limits tell you something you don't like to hear: No.

No, this isn't best. No, you don't know what is best. No is an imposition to your plans. *No* prevents you from having what you hope to have, doing what you'd love to do, or feeling the way you think you should feel. Rather than embrace the *no*, you'd like to push it away. You loathe limits and are tempted to rail against them through arguing, negotiating, forcing your way through, or denying they exist at all.

Limit-Loathers

Limits force you to come to grips with both your humanity and your sin nature by showing you that you are not God, but you sure want to be. Your spiritual parents were no different. Adam and Eve were the very first limit-loathers. God said clearly, "Of the tree of the knowledge of good and evil you *shall not* eat" (Gen. 2:17), and instead they took and ate, and ignored the limit given by God. In response, God punished their rebellion by placing them outside the garden and outside his presence. You are plagued by the same sin nature and desire to go your own way and define your own good. You want to push past limits that restrict you or tell you *no*. But heed the warning of Isaiah, "Woe to those who are wise in their own eyes, and shrewd in their own sight" (Isa. 5:21). Thankfully, there is an alternative to loathing your limits.

Check Your Blind Spots

I live on a busy street at the top of a hill. During morning and afternoon rush hour, it takes forever to get my mammoth SUV out of the driveway. Of course, I could confidently throw the car in reverse without a second thought and hope my Suburban's steel frame stops traffic and the speeding cars politely pause and let me in. But this would be foolish and would put my children's lives in danger. Instead, every time I get in a car, I acknowledge my limited perspective and look into the rearview mirror and then to my side mirrors for the perspective they can offer on whether or not it's safe to back my car out of our driveway. Without the outside input of my mirrors, every trip to Target would be a potential opportunity to total the family car.

Even though you probably don't have a driver's license yet, you do have blind spots. You can't see all your faults and insufficiencies on your own. You need an outside perspective in order to grow. You'll need to learn to ask for help. Rather than wasting your time and energy loathing every limit in your path, grow in godliness by regularly keeping check of your blind spots. Self-sufficiency is dangerous; you need the help of others. With outside input and perspective, your limitations can actually help you grow in godliness. Checking your blind spots is a sign of humility and maturity.

Yield Yourself

You were born with a major spiritual blind spot. You learned in the first chapter of this book from Ephesians 2:1–7 that you began your life *dead* in sin. Paul, knowing you'd likely forget, tells you to remember "that you were at that time separated from Christ . . . *having no hope* and without God in the world" (Eph. 2:12). You were born limited! You can't get to God on your own. You are broken by sin and have no hope of fixing yourself. This is not a limit you should argue against like the arrogant men John mentions in Revelation who say, "I am rich, I have prospered, and I need nothing," who do not realize they are "wretched, pitiable, poor, blind, and naked" (Rev. 3:17).

Without God's help, you are limited in your understanding of your need for his forgiveness, limited in your ability to trust

Christ, limited in your understanding of eternity, and limited in your ability to live for the glory of God. On your own, you cannot comprehend God's thoughts, his plans, or his purposes. You need God to give you the desire, the ability, and the strength to trust him and obey his commands. And because you are not God, you are in great need of God's wisdom in all of life. You need his help and can do nothing apart from him (John 15:5). Thankfully, your limitations and your needs do not come as a surprise to God. Whether it's personal weaknesses and inabilities or boundaries placed on you by people in authority—like your parents, your teachers, or your coach—they're all used by God for your good and his glory. He uses the same limits that annoy you or feel like a burden, to help you grow in godliness. When you admit you have blind spots and ask for God's help, the Holy Spirit responds in power, ready to assist you.

Ask for Help

How can your limits help you grow in godliness? Let's take a look at Solomon, before he became king of Israel. When his father David's time to die drew near, he commanded Solomon to "be strong, and show yourself a man, and keep the charge of the Lord your God, walking in his ways and keeping his statutes, his commandments, his rules, and his testimonies, as it is written in the Law of Moses, that you may prosper in all that you do and wherever you turn, that the Lord may establish his word" (1 Kings 2:2–4). King David charges him with the task of avenging his enemies, dealing loyally with his allies, and establishing his kingdom. Because Solomon is young and limited in experience, he needs help. When the Lord appears to him in a dream by night and asks Solomon, "What shall I give you?" Solomon responds to the Lord's invitation in this way:

You have made your servant king in place of David my father, although I am but a little child. I do not know how to go out or come in. And your servant is in the midst of your people whom you have chosen, a great people, too many to be numbered or counted for multitude. Give your servant therefore an understanding mind to govern your people, that I may discern between good and evil, for who is able to govern this your great people? (1 Kings 3:7–9)

Solomon begins with the humble admission of his limitations as the new king. He recognizes that his age and inexperience are the biggest challenges to overcome in order to govern God's people. Rather than argue or drum up a false sense of adequacy or a "fake it 'til you make it" attitude, Solomon asks for help. He acknowledges his need for God's wisdom and the ability to discern between good and evil. Solomon's response pleases the Lord (1 Kings 3:10), and so God replies:

Because you have asked this, and have not asked for yourself long life or riches or the life of your enemies, but have asked for yourself understanding to discern what is right, behold, I now do according to your word. Behold, I give you a wise and discerning mind, so that none like you has been before you and none like you shall arise after you. I give you also what you have not asked, both riches and honor, so that no other king shall compare with you, all your days. And if you will walk in my ways, keeping my statutes and my commandments, as your father David walked, then I will lengthen your days. (1 Kings 3:11–14)

God honored Solomon's humility and willingness to learn by providing him with both wisdom and honor. Where do *your* limits most often lead you? Do they direct you to greater trust and obedience to God? Or do they lead you into faithlessness, unbelief, and rebellion? When you hear a *no*, do you receive it with grace and look to the Lord for his refining wisdom? Do you ask for help? Or do you argue and complain?

You have only ever known a life of limits: bedtimes, alarm clocks, tardy bells, screen time, curfews, and age restrictions. And while limitations will look different as you grow, they won't go away. Author Jen Wilkin states that limits are a *good thing* because when we look at the limitlessness of God, who cannot be contained by time or space, wisdom or creativity, and we compare our own measly resources, we can't help but be humbled. We are different from God by design. Wilkin writes, "Our limits teach us the fear of the Lord. They are reminders that keep us from falsely believing that we can be like God."[1] Limits force us to dependence. And when we understand the source of our help, limits serve the good purpose of drawing us near to the only one capable of providing for our needs. The same God who granted Solomon wisdom continues to abound in limitless wisdom and resources today.

The Road Ahead

Carrie Underwood's *American Idol* experience was the beginning of a successful music career because she listened to feedback and submitted to the process of growth. Through all the grueling group auditions, vocal coaching sessions, and intimidating individual performances in front of live studio audiences and before the American public, Carrie had the opportunity to consider her own blind spots and respond with humility. Yielding herself to the constructive criticism and the wisdom of judges with industry experience resulted in incredible growth.

If you want to grow in godliness, recognize that you have limitations. Maturity in Christ is attained when you regularly submit yourself to God on the road to sanctification. As you stare down your own set of limitations, as annoying as they may seem, I pray that you will humbly yield to the wisdom of God and the perspective of those who love him. Ask for God's help and strength in your life, trusting that he has limitless resources and inexhaustible grace available to you. In the next three chapters, we will look at three indispensable resources God has given you to help you address your limitations and continue growing in godliness.

Grow Up by Learning from Your Limits

The mature Christian woman admits her limitations and asks God for his help and provision.

Practice Learning from Your Limits

* *Ask* God to make you aware of the limitations you most often ignore. If you're not aware of any, ask your parents or a mature Christian to help you recognize blind spots in your life.
* *Identify* ways your limitations have kept you from joyful obedience to God. Identify ways that embracing your limitations has helped you trust God.
* *Write* Psalm 84:11 as a reminder of God's promise to provide for you.
* *Pray* for humility as you learn to accept your limitations as a gift from God's hand. Ask the Spirit to help you to look outside yourself for God's mercy and provision so that you may bring him glory even in your weakness.

5

Search for Riches

Larry Page has a net worth of over forty-nine *billion* dollars, and at forty-five years old he is the sixth richest person on the globe.[1] Larry's preposterous fortune is the direct result of a dream he began cultivating as a twelve-year-old. As the son of two computer scientists, he grew up in a home filled with computers, tech magazines, and a love for electronics.[2] When he picked up a biography on the life of ingenious inventor Nikola Tesla, his own life took a clarifying turn. Larry determined then and there that he wanted to build world-changing technology.

For the next ten years, Larry studied, learned, and grew, eventually landing as a graduate student at the prestigious Stanford University. At twenty-three, he woke suddenly from a dream with a stroke of genius. He spent the remainder of the night brainstorming, scribbling down details, and strategizing how he could turn his dream into reality. He'd learned at a Michigan State summer camp that there was value in having "a healthy disregard for the impossible," and so he pressed forward against all odds. His hope? Somehow organizing all the world's information and making it universally accessible and useful. Over the next few years, with help from his friend Sergey Brin, he proceeded to develop a set of mathematical rules to systematically comb through and search every internet page on the World Wide Web. They borrowed their friends' personal computers and maxed out their credit cards buying floppy disks off the back of a truck, but the risk more than paid off. Larry and Sergey named their project *Google*.

When Google.com launched in September of 1998, it answered ten thousand search queries a day. Today, it is the most-used search engine on the market and is responsible for answering over four billion search requests a day. With very little effort, people everywhere can track powerful hurricanes looming in the ocean, educate themselves on political situations transpiring on other continents, find the lyrics to every song on the radio, and learn to use a flat iron to style their hair into perfect beach waves. Whatever we need, Google is there. Twelve-year-old Larry Page's dream became reality. Google has indeed changed our world.

Check Your Source

Thanks to Larry Page, you have extraordinary access to information. At any given moment, you can find answers to almost any question or problem you are facing as long as you have Wi-Fi. You can learn how to write a proper English essay, bake a tasty chocolate cake with ingredients you have at home, and figure out who voices the cartoon character in the movie you're watching. Very few of your questions go unanswered, leaving you with the illusion that you are indeed limitless.

In classrooms, teachers say students are most likely to look to a search engine as their primary research tool 94 percent of the time. But while the Google search bar is the top way teens gather information in today's world, it isn't the most reliable. I can't tell you how many times a Google search has been the impetus of a failed dinner recipe, a misdiagnosed illness, or a rabbit trail that ends with more questions than answers.

While Google provides endless information, it's not all accurate or trustworthy. But how do you know when to trust what it says and when to second-guess what you see on the page? Easily accessible facts and answers are no substitute for an education acquired over time through study or the expertise gained through experience. When it comes to growing in godliness, you can't Google your way to knowing God or following Christ. Not even the brilliant Larry Page can help you with that one. I guess you could say even he is #alsolimited. So where can you turn? What tools has God provided you to assist you in your limitations and help you on the road to maturity? Let's begin by looking to the Christian's primary source of wisdom, the Bible.

In a 2016 survey of your peers, 86 percent of teens agreed the Bible is a sacred text, but less than half saw it as a source of hope, and only 35 percent believed it holds everything a person needs to know to live a meaningful life.[3] These statistics reveal a heartbreaking reality: teens don't actually believe the Bible offers help for their daily lives. Recognizing that the Bible is sacred isn't enough to transform you; you must actually open it, read it, and obey it in order to grow in wisdom! Larry Page did not get into Stanford and excel in computer science because he simply knew which books he *should* read, but because he actually read them and progressed in understanding. His current success and wealth are the fruits of acquired wisdom.

Statistically speaking, you are not likely to land on Forbes's list of billionaires. But in this chapter, I would like to teach you that in order to grow in godliness you must acquire the true riches found only by cultivating biblical wisdom. The apostle Paul writes in his letter to the Colossian church of his great desire for their hearts to be encouraged to reach *all* the riches of full assurance of understanding and the knowledge of Christ, "in whom are hidden all the treasures of wisdom and knowledge" (Col. 2:3). You are wisest when your primary source of information is the Word of God, and you are richest when your greatest treasure is knowing Jesus.

Four Reasons for Searching Scripture

Who do you turn to when you need answers to your questions on life and faith? Mom and Dad? Friends? Your church youth group? Or are you among the 35 percent of teens who believe that the Bible actually *does* have everything you need?[4] Colossians 2:3 says that all the treasures of wisdom and knowledge are hidden in Christ. Truth is not hiding; it is right there in the pages of Scripture, waiting to be found. It is made plain through God's Word for all who would come and mine its depths. What are you doing to uncover this treasure in your own life? As you strive to grow in Christian maturity, here are four reasons you should search the riches of God's Holy Word.

1. The Bible Teaches You Who God Is

You learned about your best friend by spending time with her. You learned what kind of music she listened to, her favorite place to go to lunch, and which flowers make her smile, just by observation. You figured out her strengths and weaknesses, and the best parts of her character. You enjoy spending time with her because you've observed that she's a good friend. You know she's the kind of friend you can goof around with and the kind you can run to for advice.

You learn about God's character and trustworthiness by spending time with him and getting to know him in his Word. Second Samuel 22:31 says, "This God—his way is perfect; the word of the LORD proves true; he is a shield for all those who take refuge in him." It is through the counsel of his Word that you will learn to "know therefore that the LORD your God is God, the faithful God who keeps covenant and steadfast love with those who love him and keep his commandments, to a thousand generations" (Deut. 7:9). The Bible stories you read as a child aren't a series of meaningless nursery rhymes; you are old enough to know the whole story. Each of the characters in these familiar plotlines points you to aspects of God's good and perfect nature and teaches you to trust him.

In Genesis you learn that God is the good Creator, and humans are the ones who fail. In Exodus you learn that God's law is perfect, and we are imperfect covenant keepers. In Leviticus you learn about God's utter holiness and your inability to clean yourself up before God. You learn about joys and sorrows in the Psalms, wisdom in the Proverbs, and through the Prophets you learn about God's promise to deliver his people and one day set all things right. After a period of silence, Christ breaks through the darkness, and the Gospels sing of God's answer through Jesus. Paul's letters remind you to persevere in hope as you eagerly await the final return of Christ, when the bride of Christ will be restored to God forever. God's Word is his story; the more you know his story, the better you will know him.

2. The Bible Teaches You Understanding for All of Life

The Lord is a God of knowledge (1 Sam. 2:3), and in his kindness he has not withheld his wisdom. Instead, he freely "gives wisdom; from his mouth come knowledge and understanding"

(Prov. 2:6). You can find his 100 percent reliable, infallible counsel in the pages of Holy Scripture; every word is "breathed out by God and profitable for teaching, for reproof, for correction, and for training in righteousness, that the man of God may be complete, equipped for every good work" (2 Tim. 3:16–17). By simply opening the pages of the Bible, you sit at the feet of the only expert on life, gleaning knowledge from the one by whom and for whom everything and everyone was created.

Want to know how to pray? There's instruction on that. Want to know how to respond when you have problems with friends or are bullied at school? Scripture's got you. Wanting to understand God's plans for your future? It speaks to that too. Don't turn to Google; go to Scripture. Everything you need to know is right there in its pages.

3. The Bible Teaches You to Discern Right from Wrong

Scripture helps you understand God's truth so you will recognize the world's lies. Hebrews 5:13 calls everyone who is unskilled in the word of righteousness (that is, truth) childish. Maturity is attained by having your "powers of discernment trained by constant practice to distinguish good from evil" (Heb. 5:14). In order to grow up, you must leave an elementary understanding of Christ and go on to maturity (Heb. 6:1), tasting the heavenly gift, sharing in the Holy Spirit, and tasting the goodness of the Word of God and the powers of the age to come (Heb. 6:5). Pastor and author John Piper exhorts:

> Satan devotes himself 168 hours a week trying to deceive you and fill your mind with junk. He has seen to it that you are surrounded almost entirely by a Christless culture whose mood, and entertainment, and advertising, and recreation, and politics are shot through with lies about what you should

feel and think and do. Do you think that in this atmosphere you can maintain a vigorous, powerful, free, renewed mind with a ten-minute glance at God's book once a day? The reason there are church people who are basically secular like everyone else except with a religious veneer is that they devote 99% of their time to absorbing the trajectories of the world and 1% of their time to absorbing the trajectories of the Word.[5]

Piper goes on to say that in order for you to understand God and his ways, you must join yourself to his Word. This is the way you discern right from wrong. When you treat Scripture like a stranger you merely greet on the way to school and seldom spend time with, you should not be surprised "if you are ill-equipped to [understand the course] of God's will for your own life."[6]

4. The Bible Teaches You to Hope

In the introduction of this book I stated that my aim for you is that you would "grow up in every way" and no longer be a child tossed by the waves. Without a solid, biblical understanding of God's truth, you will be easily wave-thrown; sometimes it will be by life's disappointments, other times by trials, and often by your own emotions. Struggle is a part of life. If you desire to grow up in spiritual maturity and stand against the coming tidal waves of doubt, distraction, and hopelessness, you must know where to steady your hope.

Romans 5:2–5 says, "We rejoice in hope of the glory of God. Not only that, but we rejoice in our sufferings, knowing that suffering produces endurance, and endurance produces character, and character produces hope, and hope does not put us to shame, because God's love has been poured into our hearts through the Holy Spirit who has been given to us." Mature Christians prepare for what's ahead. In this case, "Preparing your minds for action, and being sober-minded, set your hope fully on the grace that will be brought to you at the revelation of Jesus Christ" (1 Pet. 1:13). You do this by dwelling in his Word.

Where will you turn in adversity and who you can trust? The psalmist writes, "For you, O Lord, are my hope, my trust, O LORD, from my youth" (Ps. 71:5). You are not too young to learn to grow in godliness by understanding God's Word and learning to hope in him. As you strive for maturity in Christ, declare with the psalmist, "For God alone, O my soul, wait in silence, for my hope is from him" (Ps. 62:5).

What Can Wisdom Buy You?

Larry Page changed the world with his wisdom by bringing the Google search bar into reality. His invention has made him rich beyond anyone's wildest imagination. With his fortune he has purchased million-dollar homes, private jets, and a forty-five-million-dollar superyacht that's equipped with a helipad, gym, and luxury suites. His wisdom changed the course of his life.

As you pursue the wisdom of God through the study of his Word, your life will radically change too. Not in the worldly way Larry's changed, but in a righteous, eternal way. God says, "Let not the rich man boast in his riches, but let him who boasts boast in this, that he understands and knows me, that I am the LORD who practices steadfast love, justice, and righteousness in the earth. For in these things I delight, declares the LORD" (Jer. 9:23–24).

Whether you live in a Christian home and are surrounded by Bibles, commentaries, and study guides of every shape and size or are the first in your family to come to faith and are just learning to seek God through his Word, you have the opportunity to let the Word of God change the course of your life. As you place yourself under God's authority, your passions and desires will change. The way you see the world will change. How you stand against criticism will change. How you love others will change. You will grow in your understanding of the Lord and desire to tell others about the good news of the gospel. God's Word will change you and shape you to look less like your natural, sinful self and more and more like Jesus every day. Grow in godliness by searching for God where he can be found: in his Word. In doing so, you will find measureless riches. Let the psalmist's words be the cry of your heart:

> How can a young [wo]man keep [her] way pure?
>> By guarding it according to your word.
> With my whole heart I seek you;
>> let me not wander from your commandments!
> I have stored up your word in my heart,
>> that I might not sin against you.
> Blessed are you, O Lord;
>> teach me your statutes!
> With my lips I declare
>> all the rules of your mouth.
> In the way of your testimonies I delight
>> as much as in all riches.
> I will meditate on your precepts
>> and fix my eyes on your ways.
> I will delight in your statutes;
>> I will not forget your word. (Ps. 119:9–16)

What will you do today, as a young teen, to ensure that the Word of God might begin to dwell richly in *you*?

Grow Up by Searching for Wisdom

The mature Christian woman resolves to look to God's Word as the source of wisdom.

Practice Searching for Wisdom

* *Ask* God to show you where you most often turn for wisdom. Is it the internet? Your parents? Your friends? Ask God to reveal ways that you've previously trusted sources other than his Word.

* *Identify* a way to daily invest in reading God's Word. Choose a Scripture reading plan and begin to work methodically through Scripture. Ask a parent, mentor, or friend to hold you accountable to identify a plan and begin reading.

* *Write* 2 Timothy 3:16–17 on a Post-it Note and place it next to your bed as a reminder to regularly search Scripture as your first source for wisdom.

* *Pray* through Psalm 119:9–16 before you read each day and ask the Lord to store up his Word in your heart as you read. As you pray each day, work toward committing this scriptural prayer to memory. Ask God to give you a growing desire for "the word of Christ" to "dwell in you richly" (Col. 3:16). Ask him to help you turn to Scripture for wisdom, encouragement, and hope.

6

Love His Church

For as long as I can remember, my son Jude has *loved* the salad bar at Jason's Deli. He begs to eat there whenever we are in the area, and each year he chooses Jason's for his birthday dinner. With eyes bigger than his stomach, he grabs an empty plate and heads to the back right corner of the salad bar, preparing to feast. Ironically, he has zero interest in vegetables. Lettuce, tomatoes, cucumbers—yuck—he'll pass. He chooses the salad bar and places none of the healthy options on his plate. Why then, does he love the salad bar? Because hidden in the back right corner there sits a bountiful basket of gingerbread minimuffins. It's not the salad bar he loves. It's the sugary appetizers in the back. If the muffins disappeared, he wouldn't love the salad bar at all.

As a "Gen Z" teenager, you are surrounded by people who call themselves Christians in the same way I call my son a salad-lover. They say they love Jesus, but they don't love the church. Statistically speaking, more than half of your generation see involvement in the church as unimportant, and only 20 percent regard it as "very important."[1] According to research, teens tend to think they can find God elsewhere or that church is just not relevant to them personally.[2] The majority of your peers feel the same way about the church as my son feels about eating vegetables. It might be beneficial, but it sure isn't desirable or necessary.

It's understandable. Without ever involving the church, you could look to God's Word for wisdom, identify a few Christian friends, read good Christian books, listen to Christian music, and pretend the only pastor you need is a podcast. Why not outsource the role of the church and tutor yourself in Christian maturity? In an interview, Pastor John Piper addresses this recent phenomenon of people who say they love Jesus but are done with the church:

> To say, "I love Jesus, but I don't submit to his word" is a lie. "If anyone loves me, he will keep my word" (John 14:23). Jesus founded the church. . . . So the choice of Jesus over church implies a choice of your opinion over the Bible, because the Bible is where we meet Jesus. You can't make Jesus up. . . . He is the Jesus of the Bible or he is the Jesus of your imagination. If he is the Jesus of the Bible, you take the whole Jesus. You can't carve him up in pieces. And the whole Jesus is the Jesus who loves the church. He died for the church.[3]

In this chapter, I want to show you that just as you can't say you love the salad bar and hate veggies, neither can you say you love Jesus without loving his church. The church is another necessary means of God's grace in your life, a helpful tool used to conform you to Christlikeness. And as we look to Scripture, I'm confident you'll find the church not only necessary, but gloriously worthy of your pursuit.

What Is the Church?

When you think of the church, what do you picture? Is the picture in your mind a building with a steeple and stained-glass windows? Or a small country church with a few pews and a piano at the front? Maybe it's a mobile setup in your local elementary school cafeteria. Or do you think of your Sunday morning experience? Do you think of how trendy the music sounds, how funny the pastor's jokes are, or whether his messages seem relevant to your daily life? Perhaps you think of the people. Maybe you think of Aunt Stella who can't hear but is still playing the piano, or the youth group you spend Wednesday nights with, or the pastor who your parents love but you just don't connect with. Is your love for the church based on the presence of steeples, the style of the sermon, or the musical stylings of Stella? Or is there more to the church than buildings, experiences, and peoples' preferences? In order to *love* the church, you must *know* the church.

The church you are called to love is a *people*. All those who were once far off have been brought near through the sacrifice of Jesus and are now "fellow citizens with the saints and members of the household of God, built on the foundation of the apostles and prophets, Christ Jesus himself being the cornerstone, in whom the whole structure, being joined together, grows into a holy temple in the Lord. In him you also are being built together into a dwelling place for God by the Spirit" (Eph. 2:19–22). The people of God are bigger than cafeterias or cathedrals, and the construction project they're currently under is more massive than any multimillion dollar building campaign. If you are alive in Christ, you are one brick in the new church God is building on the foundation of his Son! Like a living brick, you are being built into the spiritual house (1 Pet. 2:5), the body of Christ, the *church*. Pastor and teacher R. C. Sproul put it this way:

The church is a new temple built in Christ, by Christ, and for Christ. Obviously, Paul isn't saying the church is a building made out of mortar and brick, but that we are the stones, the living stones, as 1 Peter 2:5 tells us. Each believer is part of this church just as each stone is part of a building. The church, the new temple, is still under construction. Every day, new stones are added. This new temple will not be finished until Jesus returns to consummate His kingdom. Christ is still building His church, not by adding cement but by adding people who are the stones that hold together in Him.[4]

Every day, God is adding to the building. New believers become part of the church without even rolling out of bed, getting in the car, or walking into the church building on Sunday morning; they are part of the church simply because God made them alive in Christ. If you are a believer, you are a part of the body of Christ and individually a member of it (1 Cor. 12:27). We are "fellow heirs, members of the same body, and partakers of the promise in Christ Jesus through the gospel" (Eph. 3:6), and together with the rest of the members of the household of God, we make up "the church of the living God, a pillar and buttress of the truth" (1 Tim. 3:15). This full-bodied representation of God's people is often referred to as the universal church. I like to call it the "Big *C* Church." Here are three glorious truths about the Big *C* Church:

- *The church is eternal.* The church includes followers of Christ throughout all generations (Eph. 3:21): the disciples whose letters you find in the Bible, the missionaries you've read about who died before you were born, and the saints you meet in Sunday morning worship. Each are a part of the eternal church. The church also includes all people who will one day come to saving faith.

- *The church is global.* The church is made up of people of every tribe, language, people, and nation (Rev. 5:9). Though separated across waters, continents, and cultures, the beautifully diverse family of God is united as one under the salvation of Christ.
- *The church is local.* You connect to the universal, eternal, and global church by connecting to your local church. That is where you learn to walk by faith alongside other believers. Meeting together locally—to hear God's Word preached, make disciples, baptize new believers, observe the Lord's Supper, pray, sing, fellowship, and worship the living God as one body under Christ—has been a priority to professing Christians for almost two thousand years. Whether meeting in homes, countryside churches, or large stained-glass sanctuaries, Christians have valued togetherness with the church.

How does your previous idea of *what* the church is compare with God's vision for *who* the church is? Perhaps you've been guilty of unintentionally underestimating the church's glory and grandeur. But when you catch a glimpse of it from God's perspective, the church is extremely relevant; centuries later it still speaks and testifies through God's Holy Word in order to guide and direct the world to God's truth and the gospel of Jesus Christ. The church is the city on the hill shining in darkness (Matt. 5:14). God will not be found apart from Christ, and Christ will not be found apart from his church.

What Does the Church Have to Offer?

Let's return to the salad bar at Jason's Deli. Would I love for Jude to eat from the fullness of the salad bar? Absolutely. Crisp green cucumbers. Ripe red radishes. Leafy green lettuce. I know they all have delicious, nutritious, healthy benefits that far surpass those of the minimuffins he'd rather gorge himself on. At home, I attempt to persuade him to eat his veggies because they're good for his body. The church is similar. You must step away from the pick-and-choose mentality and learn to value every healthy piece, for the good of the body. Author Brett McCracken addresses this immature tendency:

> For too long the consumer logic of Christian culture has been: Find a church that meets your needs! Find a church were the worship music moves you, the pastor's preaching compels you, and the homogenous community welcomes you! You, you, you! . . . A true gospel community is not about convenience and comfort and chai lattes in the vestibule. It's about pushing each other forward in holiness and striving together for the kingdom, joining along in the ongoing work of the Spirit in this world. Those interested only in their comfort and happiness need not apply. Being the church is difficult.[5]

Yes, like eating your vegetables, committing to love and enjoy messy, broken, sinful people seems way less appealing than avoiding them. But you need to value God's people and commit to being around them for your spiritual nourishment and growth in godliness.

"Christ loved the church and gave himself up for her, *that he might sanctify her*, having cleansed her by the washing of water with the word, so that he might present the church to himself in splendor, without spot or wrinkle or any such thing, that she might be holy and without blemish" (Eph. 5:25–27). This means our faith is not an "every woman for herself" situation. If Christ desires a purified body, we should too. To that end, we must be prepared to see our pursuit of holiness not as a work-from-home project, but as a community effort! We must love working for holiness together as the church.

Consider how many times God's Word commends you to obedience through "one another" commands. To *love* one another, you must be around one another and know one another. To *forgive* one another, you must be around one another to be sinned against. To *submit* to one another, you must disagree with one another. To *encourage* one another, you must be familiar with the discouragements of one another (1 Thess. 5:11). To *exhort* one another, you must see the deficiencies and errors in one another (Heb. 3:13). To *stir up* one another to good works, you must recognize idleness in one another (Heb. 10:24). To *confess* your sins to one another, you must have relationships with one another (James 5:16).

In chapter 4 we discussed limitations and the need for God's help to grow in godliness. Your local church is designed to help facilitate that growth. Inside the church, God provides you pastors and elders to joyfully watch over your soul (Heb. 13:17), teachers and defenders of the truth to keep you from swerving from the faith (1 Tim. 6:21), and countless testimonies of witnesses commending you to run the race of faith (Heb. 11:2). When you are faithless, the church reminds you of God's track record of faithfulness to his people. When you doubt God's willingness to provide for you, the church declares all God has done. When you face whatever persecution and severe affliction God allows in your path, there's fellowship among others who are also suffering in Christ's name.

The church is God's glorious provision for weak and needy followers of Christ. Better than a forgettable building, a useless gimmick, or a weekly gathering that's overlooked, the church is a people deemed indispensable by Christ and therefore worthy of your affection. The church is gloriously good for you. Pray that you would look forward to spending your Sunday with God's people. Seat yourself in the cafeteria chair or church pew and joyfully participate in the family of God.

What Should I Bring to Church?

As a pastor's wife, I frequently invite people I meet to attend our church. One of the first things I'm asked is "What should I bring to church?" They want to know if they're supposed to bring a snack to share, their own copy of the Bible, or money for the offering plate. I appreciate their attempts at preparation. As a teenager in the church, it's important to prepare yourself to come to church as the vital, necessary, contributing member of the body of Christ that you are.

Bring humility. Leave your preferences, entitlements, and disappointments at the door and enter with humility. "Likewise, you who are younger, be subject to the elders. Clothe yourselves, all of you, with humility toward one another, for 'God opposes the proud but gives grace to the humble'" (1 Pet. 5:5).

Bring a readiness to serve. "For even the Son of Man came not to be served but to serve, and to give his life as a ransom for many" (Mark 10:45). Your Sunday morning church attendance and ongoing participation in your local body of gathered believers is not only for the purpose of growing, but also for *serving.* You are a fellow worker in God's church, working to build God's temple (1 Cor. 3:9), and there is kingdom work to be done. Take the form of a servant.

Bring compassion. "God's love has been poured into our hearts through the Holy Spirit" (Rom. 5:5), and in response we are called to love one another with brotherly affection, outdoing one another in showing honor (Rom. 12:10). Our love must be genuine inside the church in order to be noticed outside the church.

Bring your gifts. "As each has received a gift, use it to serve one another, as good stewards of God's varied grace" (1 Pet. 4:10). God wants to use the gifts he's given you not as an opportunity for your own glory, but for the building up of the body. You are one member of the greater body with an important role to play (Rom. 12:6).

Love the Church

Do you long to grow in godliness? Go to church. Get to know the church. Learn to love the church. Start this Sunday by setting your alarm clock and going joyfully. Be among the few in your generation who consider church involvement very important. Prioritize your weekly commitment to God's people because you believe the church body is an indispensable part of the Christian's life. As a follower of Christ you have the weekly privilege of joining in spirit with brothers and sisters across the globe, to express gratitude and praise to Jesus together as they have done for centuries.

Just as those who love the salad bar love veggies, those who love Jesus love his church. And even though I just compared the importance of participating in his body to eating your vegetables, loving God's people and meeting together is exponentially more delightful than cucumbers. The church is a means of God's grace in your life, assisting you in your conformity to Christlikeness. Grow in godliness by growing in your love for Christ's church.

Grow Up by Loving Christ's Church

The mature Christian woman loves and commits to the body of Christ.

Practice Loving Christ's Church

* *Ask* yourself how invested you are in loving your local church. Do your actions and attitudes demonstrate apathy or appreciation? Have your affections for the church been formed by the world or by God's Word?

* *Identify* ways the Holy Spirit might be calling you to grow in your desires to be around God's people. Identify ways to spend more time and energy investing in your church.

* *Write* a text or an email to a member of your church whom you love and respect, asking if she would be willing to disciple you. Don't be afraid to think outside your age range—I regularly look to saints who are older and have more life experience. If you can't think of anyone, ask your parents or your pastor to connect you with someone trustworthy.

* *Pray* for God to use you during your teen years to build and strengthen his church for the day of Christ's return. Ask him to use your life and love for the church to make his name known in the world, and to empower you to set an example for the believers "in speech, in conduct, in love, in faith, [and] in purity" (1 Tim. 4:12).

Pray Continually

Around Spring Branch Community Church in Houston, Texas, Pauline Tallula Tate was the prime portrait of a praying woman. Sure, she'd pray at home on her own. But she'd also pray in the parking lot, in the ladies' room, in the back of a worship service, in hallways, classrooms, and any other nook or cranny she could find. When Mama Tate said, "I'll pray for you," she didn't just mean whenever it happened to cross her mind; she meant right now with you and later on her own. Her sparklingly expectant eyes danced each time she clasped a friend's hand in an invitation: "Let's just pray about that right now!" She knew her wisdom and counsel were limited, so she'd rather close her eyes and talk to Jesus. When Mama Tate spoke, out of her heart flowed rivers of living water (John 7:38).

At eighty-one years old Mama Tate joined the digital world of Facebook, and her prayers spilled over to the internet. She used her social media status updates to pray for her children, grandchildren, church friends, missionaries, foreign students she'd given Bibles to, and anyone else who'd read and pray along. She also used it to ask for prayer: "We have a problem. Poison Ivy. Pray how to proceed." To Mama Tate, no prayer request was too small.

A few years later Mama Tate faced cancer and a broken back after a bad fall. Rather than pity herself, she saw her health crisis as a missionary journey; she'd been appointed to serve in hospital rooms and skilled nursing facilities. She went on to pray for and share Christ with over two hundred doctors, nurses, and patients. Near the end of her life her doctor said, "Mama Tate, you are losing weight and energy and probably have less than six months to live, but your countenance is more radiant than ever!" As she'd prayed Numbers 6:24–26—"The LORD bless and keep you; the LORD make his face to shine upon you and be gracious to you; the LORD lift up his countenance upon you and give you peace"—countless times for others, the Holy Spirit had transformed her heart.

When Mama Tate passed away, her son said her greatest legacy was teaching her children the importance of prayer. At her funeral, he asked for everyone who'd been personally prayed for by Mama Tate to stand. In the room of five hundred people, around 90 percent stood in testimony to the faithful legacy of a woman who found prayer essential. I was honored to be one of the friends standing that day, testifying to her life's dependence on prayer. How had Mama Tate's life become so filled with the Spirit of God, ever flowing with fresh wisdom from the Word, and abounding with joy and confidence in her salvation through Jesus? My guess? Through prayer.

Wimpy, Wimpy Prayer Life

In comparison to Mama Tate, my own prayer life seemed embarrassingly wimpy. If you feel this way, don't despair. Just as you must grow in godliness by studying God's Word, you must also grow in godliness by practicing the discipline of prayer. It takes time and work to develop a mature prayer life. Christians don't come to faith in Christ and immediately lay hold of a robust and confident prayer life like Mama Tate's.

It is far more common for the young believer's prayers to feel lackluster, robotic, monotonous, lifeless, and insecure. Initially, it may feel unnatural to talk to someone you cannot see and to wait for him to answer without audible words, for some unknown amount of time. When you don't understand prayer, you will avoid praying, and not surprisingly, your prayers will remain wimpy and immature. Here are a few telltale ways a wimpy prayer life often manifests:

- *Demanding Baby*: using prayers only to get what you want from God
- *Fair-Weather Friend*: praying only when convenient or in need
- *Superstitious*: praying as a means of avoiding something bad happening
- *Dodging*: avoiding personal prayer by praying for random things like Grandma's cat, your neighbor's mom's sister, or the weather
- *God Bless Mama*: praying in monotonous list form
- *Rub-a-Dub-Dub*: praying memorized prayers quickly before eating
- *Dozer*: praying for two minutes before dozing off to sleep.

If you can relate, it's ok. We all begin somewhere. Remember from chapter 4: acknowledging your limitations and humbly admitting your wimpy or undeveloped prayer life is a good starting point. But don't get comfy here. As you grow in godliness, your prayers will grow and become more and more like the powerful petitions of Jesus.

Don't settle for only bedtime and mealtime prayers spoken by your parents. Are your prayers powerful, trusting, and anticipatory? Is praying a joy and a privilege? Start by admitting your need for growth. Set the bar higher than it is today. Aim to speak with God in a way that displays tenacious trust and counts on his readiness to respond to every request. A *dependent* prayer life is a sign of maturity in the life of the believer. If you aren't there today, take heart and set your heart, mind, and prayers on growth.

Teach Me to Pray

At the risk of sounding redundant, Scripture is the best place to learn how to pray. Remember, it's the source of all wisdom. It is filled with the testimonies of God's people and their dependence on talking to God through prayer in all sorts of situations. Abraham prayed to God and saw Abimelech and his wife healed (Gen. 20:17). Isaac prayed for his wife, and Rebekah conceived (Gen. 25:21). Moses prayed when Pharaoh refused to free the Israelites (Ex. 8:30). Jonah prayed from the belly of the fish even when his own rebellion had landed him there (Jonah 2:1). King David cried out to God in prayer through weakness and strength, both weeping and rejoicing. Each of these men lifted up prayers to God in faith because they knew God would hear and respond. You can trust the Lord's promise: "You will call upon me and come and pray to me, and I will hear you" (Jer. 29:12).

As a follower of Christ, prayer is the way you communicate with God. In Matthew 6:5–7, Jesus doesn't instruct his disciples to rely on prayer only if they're inclined to find it helpful. He trusts they understand the importance of prayer as generations before had, and then dives right into instructing them on *how* to do it. Jesus says, *"when you pray"* because he expects his disciples to communicate with the Father through the means of prayer. He goes on to offer further instruction to his disciples in Matthew 6:6–8:

> When you pray, go into your room and shut the door and pray to your Father who is in secret. And your Father who sees in secret will reward you.
>
> And when you pray, do not heap up empty phrases as the Gentiles do, for they think that they will be heard for their many words. Do not be like them, for your Father knows what you need before you ask him.

Then, he gives the disciples the same thing we need today—a picture of what prayer should look like. He says, "Pray then like this":

> Our Father in heaven,
> hallowed be your name.
> Your kingdom come,
> your will be done,
>   on earth as it is in heaven.
> Give us this day our daily bread,
> and forgive us our debts,
>   as we also have forgiven our debtors.
> And lead us not into temptation,
>   but deliver us from evil. (Matt. 6:9–13)

Jesus offers this model prayer for more than memory work. It is a template teaching you to pray in mature, God-honoring, Christ-exalting ways. Rather than a repetitive recipe to recite, it's meant to guide you to growth in your prayer life and bring you closer to Christlike dependence on your Father.

The Lord's prayer strengthens your prayers by teaching you to rightly approach God:

- *"Our Father in heaven" teaches sonship.* As a child of God, you have access to your Father through Jesus, and can come to him as his adopted, beloved child. Confessing God as your Father also reminds you of his place of authority over the world at large and more personally, over your life. Praying to God as Father reminds you that because of the gospel, your Father is compassionate and near when you pray.
- *"Hallowed be your name" teaches reverence.* Though God is your Father, he is also the Lord of Hosts. "Holy, holy, holy"—the whole earth is filled with his glory (Isa. 6:3). Prayer ascribes to your Creator and Redeemer the glory due his name (1 Chron. 16:29). When Jesus offered up prayers with loud cries and tears, he was heard because of his reverence (Heb. 5:7). Praying with reverence ensures your prayers are heard.
- *"Your kingdom come, your will be done, on earth as it is in heaven" teaches submission.* While God hears reverent prayers, he isn't bound to answer in the way you'd like. Jesus understood that his Father's desires for his kingdom took precedence over his own. Remember his sovereign goodness that we learned about in chapter 3? When Jesus prayed in the garden before his crucifixion, he cried, "My Father, if it be possible, let this cup pass from me; nevertheless, not as I will, but as you will" (Matt. 26:39). Prayerful submission helps you to confess your limited perspective and reminds you of God's good and sovereign control of all things.
- *"Give us this day our daily bread" teaches dependence.* God is your provider and sustainer. "He provides food

for those who fear him; he remembers his covenant forever" (Ps. 111:5). Prayer helps you remember that just as he provided the Israelites daily manna in the desert, he continues to provide for you through his living Word, his Spirit, and through tangible provisions like the food on your table and the bed you sleep in each night. Prayers of dependence remind you of the source from which your help comes.

- *"Forgive us our debts, as we also have forgiven our debtors" teaches forgiveness.* Forgiveness is an ongoing endeavor for the believer. "Blessed is the one whose transgression is forgiven, whose sin is covered" (Ps. 32:1). And you must share the blessing of forgiveness with others. Your Father will forgive you *if* you forgive others, but if you do not forgive others, neither will your Father forgive you (Matt. 6:14–15). Your prayers not only remind you of the debt that Christ paid on your behalf, but they remind you to be proactive in forgiving others.

- *"Lead us not into temptation, but deliver us from evil" teaches humility.* Jesus instructed the disciples to "watch and pray that [they] may not enter into temptation. The spirit is indeed willing, but the flesh is weak" (Matt. 26:41). It is the Lord who keeps you from the evil one (John 17:15). God will rescue you from every evil deed and bring you safely into his heavenly kingdom (2 Tim. 4:18). Admitting weakness and asking for God's protection against the enemy's schemes teaches you humility in the midst of temptation as you wait on the Lord's final deliverance.

You will not naturally stumble into a mature prayer life that expresses the delight of sonship, holy reverence for God, kingdom submission, dependence on his provision, forgiveness for those who've wronged you, and humility in your weakness. These marks of Christlike maturity come with time, determination, and lots of practice.

Getting It Right

Mama Tate's public prayer life was an extension of her personal prayer life. She found joy in approaching the throne of grace on her own and couldn't wait to share the joy with others. Her prayers had an air of confidence because she'd spent years experiencing God's faithfulness. By the time her soft arthritic hand clasped mine in prayer, she didn't fumble for words or stall while figuring out what to say next. Her thoughtful prayers were the fruit of years of growing in godliness.

As you learn to pray the way Jesus taught his disciples, expect some bumps. You won't sound like the practiced eighty-year-old. When my children were young, I would often ask them to pray out loud before bed. They'd argue and say "No, you pray!" They worried they'd say the wrong thing or that it wouldn't be good enough. Many adults still share these fears. But the desire for perfection, or to appear mature before you've had a chance to develop maturity, must not keep you from approaching the Father in prayer. Just get started!

The apostle Paul instructs you to "pray without ceasing" (1 Thess. 5:17), at all times making requests of God (Eph. 6:18), in order to stay alert with all perseverance, being watchful with thanksgiving (Col. 4:2). You need God's help to persevere in the faith! Prayer helps to keep you from losing heart (Luke 18:1), and it enables you to have strength to escape the coming trials of life (Luke 21:36). In order to grow in godliness, you must depend on prayer. The act of prayer is humbling; it confesses your need for God's help and the reliance on him to provide what you cannot provide for yourself.

When is the last time you asked someone to pray for you? Have you taken the time to pray on your own? Start today by taking every need, desire, worry, or burden to the feet of Jesus. You can pray on the bus on the way home from school, in your room at your desk, or at the kitchen table with your mom. Start praying and don't ever stop.

In Luke 18, Jesus tells the parable of the widow petitioning an unrighteous judge for justice against her adversary: "For a while he refused, but afterward he said to himself, 'Though I neither fear God nor respect man, yet because this widow keeps bothering me, I will give her justice, so that she will not beat me down by her continual coming'" (Luke 18:4–5). Jesus continues, "And will not God give justice to his elect, who cry to him day and night? Will he delay long over them? I tell you, he will give justice to them speedily" (Luke 18:7–8). As you strive to grow in godliness, cry to God in prayer as fervently as the pestering widow. Day and night, beat down his door, continually coming like my dear, sweet friend, Mama Tate. The eyes of the Lord are on you, the righteous, and his ears are open to your prayer (1 Pet. 3:12).

Grow Up by Praying Continually

The mature Christian woman expresses dependence on God through her continual prayers.

Practice Praying Continually

* *Ask* yourself how much you've depended on prayer in the last week, month, or year. Do you regularly find comfort in prayer? Why or why not?
* *Identify* three areas of your life that you'd like to commit to pray over in the next week.
* *Write* out Psalm 143:1, and underneath write the three areas you've committed to pray over.
* *Pray* for God to give you a desire to pray and regularly seek his face. Pray that God would strengthen your prayers through an awareness of your sonship, giving you a reverence for his holiness, a submission to his kingdom plans, dependence on his provision, a willingness to forgive, and a desire to flee from evil.

Part 3

MONITOR YOUR GROWTH

8

Use Your Words

Doctor check-ups are good for more than lollipops, although my daughter often needs convincing. Once a year we argue over the necessity of her annual visit to the pediatrician. As *Dora the Explorer* cartoons play in the background of the waiting room, the nurse ushers Madeline back, records her weight and height, and hands her the dreaded paper gown. Under protest, she changes and then perches on the exam table. Her legs swing anxiously as she waits for what seems like an eternity for the pediatrician to poke, prod, and examine her. These appointments seem like an inconvenience because there are usually no surprises; we're able to confirm she's growing right on target for her age.

This hasn't always been the case. I remember the day I cradled our tiny four-month-old daughter in pink blankets at one not-so-routine check-up. That day the pediatrician's brow furrowed as she looked at the facts. Madeline hadn't gained weight over the past few weigh-ins; she wasn't growing the way she should have.

The pediatrician scribbled the words "failure to thrive" on her chart and then proceeded to advise me on what this diagnosis meant for the weeks ahead. As a first-time mother, I'd missed the signs and symptoms. Thankfully, monitoring her weight and growth helped us evaluate the problem and begin working to restore her health. By God's grace, her body responded, and today she's as healthy as ever.

As you grow, routine physical check-ups serve as a helpful snapshot of your health. Are you growing and developing as expected? Or, do you need a little outside intervention? As a Christian, your spiritual health also benefits from regular check-ups. In chapter 1, we discussed that you are a work-in-progress, awaiting full redemption. You are not yet the picture of Christ that you will one day become. Until you are fully made like Christ, you must strive to *grow in godliness*. If you are alive in Christ, godliness will be increasing (2 Pet. 1:8). How can you monitor your spiritual health and growth?

In part 2 of this book you learned about three tools God provides to facilitate your growth in godliness: God's Word, his church, and prayer. In this final section I want to encourage you to monitor your growth in godliness by looking to a few easily observable measures of growth: your words, your emotions, and your fruit. Each are indicators of healthy growth in godliness along the path to maturity in Christ. As you invest time in God's Word, spend time with God's people, and seek God's wisdom through prayer, the Holy Spirit—the Great Physician that he is—will lovingly poke and prod, encouraging you toward growth.

Use Your Words

Words have a way of pointing to what's inside our hearts. As my toddlers learn to talk, one of the first, most basic instructions I teach them is the phrase "use your words." Don't hit your sister; *use your words*. Don't scream at Daddy; *use your words*. Stop crying, and help me understand; *use your words*. As they learn to speak, they learn that words help them communicate their thoughts, feelings, and needs to those around them. And yet, even as they grow in their ability to voice their concerns through words, they haven't yet developed maturity and self-control inside their small, sin-crooked hearts. The angry toddler who once hit his sister now *uses his words* to angrily yell at his sister. Instead of thrashing wildly as their dad picks them up to take them to time out, they *use their words* to protest: "No! No time out!" They're using their words, all right. They just aren't using them with maturity.

Christians experience similar growing pains. We use our words to demonstrate what's inside our hearts, but they don't always show the fruit of the Spirit. Sometimes our words demonstrate stubborn sin and immaturity. God has generously given us the ability to speak and communicate for *his* purposes: to praise him, to obey him, to live peaceably with one another, to share the gospel, to teach and exhort others to godliness, to bless others, and to express love and compassion. And yet it's a constant challenge to use our words in ways that please and honor him. Because we've been called to do everything to the glory of God (1 Cor. 10:31), our tongues should pour out speech that is gracious and obedient to God. So, why does this seem so hard and sometimes downright impossible?

As a young teenager, my speech didn't reflect a heart that had been changed by the gospel. I criticized others when it made me look better. I was bitingly sarcastic toward my friends. I taunted my younger brother. I belittled others behind their backs. I gossiped. I lied. I twisted stories in order to make myself look innocent when I wasn't. I argued with my parents. I cursed when I thought it made me look cool, even though it didn't. My words painted a picture of immaturity and rebellion, not submission to Christ.

Why was it so hard to use my words in ways that honored God? James 3:8–10 says, "No human being can tame the tongue. It is a restless evil, full of deadly poison. With it we bless our Lord and Father, and with it we curse people who are made in the likeness of God. From the same mouth come blessing and cursing." But this disappointing reality is not an excuse to give our tongues free rein. We know this because James also warns, "My brothers, these things ought not to be so." As you grow in godliness, use your words to help you take measure of increasing Christian maturity.

Measure Maturity

Your words act as a natural measure of your progression in Christian maturity because they are a direct reflection of your increasing submission to Christ and the heart change that follows. Think of a young believer who is new to the faith. Is she immediately a fountain of hope, faith, and trust in Christ? Or does it take time for her words to begin reflecting obedience to Christ? Now, think of a mature Christian you love and respect. Does she constantly gossip, lie, and curse? Or do her words encourage, set an example of faith, and challenge others to live a life of loving obedience to Christ? As you are conformed to Christ, your words will reflect the change, for all to see and hear. If you struggle to use your words in ways that honor God, consider the words of Jesus:

> How can you speak good, when you are evil? For out of the abundance of the heart the mouth speaks. The good person out of his good treasure brings forth good, and the evil person out of his evil treasure brings forth evil. I tell you, on the day of judgment people will give account for every careless word

they speak, for by your words you will be justified, and by your words you will be condemned. (Matt. 12:34–37)

We can't help but pour out what's inside. Before your salvation, you were dead in sin and your words condemned you. They did not reflect *good* treasure because you had none inside yourself. But once God makes you alive in Christ, the Spirit begins to address every inch of underlying evil—all your careless thoughts and desires—encouraging you to work toward putting all sin to death. In order to address your words, you must first address your heart. As one author writes:

> For good or bad, for better or worse, our words reveal what's in our hearts—because that's where they begin. They are signs or "symptoms" of our heart's condition. If our hearts are tender, merciful, and compassionate, our words will show it. If we've been nurturing the fruit of the Spirit, that fruit will be evident in the things we say as well as the things we do. Conversely, if our hearts are self-centered and self-focused, if they are hard and callused, if they are bitter or greedy or envious or proud, our words will reveal that too.[1]

If you were to examine your words, putting them through a spiritual health check-up, what signs or symptoms would you find? Would your words show evidence of a tender, merciful, and compassionate heart? Or would they point to selfishness, anger, or bitterness? And let's not stop with spoken words; what about the words you type and text? If it's "out of the abundance of the heart the mouth speaks" (Matt. 12:34), then you can trust that out of the abundance of the heart, the fingers also type and text. How do you speak, type, text, and communicate with your family, friends, neighbors, and teachers? Do your words display maturity or immaturity? While I've certainly grown leaps and bounds over the years, my words still display evidences of both. I still need the Spirit's conviction and help to grow in godliness when my words point to existing immaturity.

If you've used your words to measure your maturity and you recognize that you, too, have an ongoing need to change and grow, where should you begin?

Do Your Part

All this measuring and observation is useless if you do nothing with your findings. In order to change and grow, you must also do your part. James 3:6 says, "The tongue is a fire, a world of unrighteousness." Uncontrolled fires cause massive destruction and need to be extinguished quickly. When your words are inconsistent with the commands of Christ, you must take the blazing fire seriously and ask for God's help. James goes on to say, "'God opposes the proud but gives grace to the humble.' *Submit* yourselves therefore to God. *Resist* the devil, and he will flee from you. *Draw near* to God, and he will draw near to you.... *Humble* yourselves before the Lord, and he will exalt you" (4:6–8, 10). God does his part, providing grace and drawing near to you. And you must do your part, humbly submitting to God, resisting temptation, and continually drawing near to God.

You have an active role in controlling the sinful blaze of your tongue. In Psalm 34:1 the psalmist instructs you to "*keep* your tongue from evil and your lips from speaking deceit." In Psalm 39:1 he says, "I will *guard* my ways, that I may not sin with my tongue." In Proverbs we are told that "whoever *guards* his mouth preserves his life" (13:13) and "*keeps himself* out of trouble" (21:23). Like the psalmist, humble yourself and draw near to God, pleading with him to help you in these endeavors: "Set a guard, O LORD, over my mouth; keep watch over the door of my lips! Do not let my heart incline to any evil" (Ps. 141:3–4). Use your words as a regular heart check-up.

Use your words to monitor your growth in godliness, and work with God to make them more clearly reflect Christ. As you partner with the powerful Holy Spirit, who's faithfully at work in you, your heart will change and grow. With time, your words will reveal a heart that's healthier than ever.

Grow Up by Using Your Words

The mature Christian woman sees the holiness of her words as a reflection of the holiness of her heart and strives for continued growth in purity.

Practice Using Your Words

✽ *Ask* a few of your closest friends what your words say about you and what you believe. Do you use your words differently than your non-Christian friends? Ask for examples. (You should begin by asking a Christian friend, but it might also be helpful to ask a friend who isn't a follower of Jesus.)

✽ *Identify* any areas of your speech that do not reflect the character of Christ. Do your words reveal a lack of trust, gratitude, or respect? Are you careless with your words or do you engage in gossip or use your words to cut down others?

✽ *Write* Psalm 141:3 and place it where you'll see it regularly. Commit it to memory so you can use it as a prayer when you're tempted to sin against God with your words.

✽ *Pray* for God to give you a renewed passion for using your words to love and serve his kingdom. Ask him to convict you by his Spirit when your words reveal sin and brokenness inside. Pray for God to use the words of his saints to challenge, convict, and encourage you in your growth in godliness.

9

Steward Your Feelings

I will never forget the first time I experienced the thunderous crash and downpour of my historically even-tempered daughter's pent-up teenage feelings. A teenager's emotions can be as unpredictable as a sudden summer thunderstorm; one minute they're sunny and cheerful, and the next minute they've turned dark and ominous. All had been calm and quiet as we talked casually over the laundry we were folding. As our conversation continued, things grew a little tense, and I glanced up to see Madeline's eyes brimming with tears. Concerned and caught off-guard by the sudden change of emotion, I asked her what was bothering her. She couldn't tell me. She shrugged, burst into tears, and said with embarrassment, "I just feel like crying, and I don't even know why!"

I suppose I should have stopped right then and there and issued her some kind of official welcome into Club Womanhood, where one's membership privileges include learning to navigate a new world of strong and often unpredictable emotions. Instead, I gave her a cookie and a listening ear. As a teenager, you're likely entering the club too, and you must understand that while your emotions are indeed strong and unpredictable, you are not a damsel in distress, forced to regularly surrender to their powerful sway. You'll need more than cookies to face your feelings; you'll need wisdom and maturity.

Why, as women, are we so quick to let our feelings lead? Admittedly, answering this question could become a book in itself. For our purposes in this chapter, I want to examine one specifically misleading message that often stands in the way of a teenager's maturity. Chances are you've heard it heralded through the halls of your schools and seen it brandished on backpacks, and perhaps you've even sung versions of its message as it plays on the radio.

Be who you want to be. Live your truth. You do you. Follow your heart. Your generation champions the freedom to follow your heart on television shows, inside library books, and in everyday conversations with friends. These "motivational" messages are printed on posters in your pediatrician's office, spoken in the lunch line of your school cafeteria, and worn proudly on T-shirts. These messages tell you that your emotions and feelings matter more than logic, reasoning, or understanding, and especially more than the absolute truth of Scripture. Their self-prioritizing messages tempt you to *follow your heart*, even when doing so means disobeying God's commands.

While the message of *follow your heart* may be the natural and popular cry of the teenage girl's heart, it isn't the key to unlocking holiness. So rather than settling into natural teenage tendencies or excusing your moodiness, let's consider how following your heart can wreak havoc on your growth in godliness.

Stop Following Your Heart

Though the message of *follow your heart* is written into nearly all your favorite fairy tales, the message shouldn't be instructive for the Christ-follower. Following your heart rarely results in a happy ending. I've followed my heart into some pretty embarrassing and sinful predicaments that held consequences instead of a tidy bow. As a teenager, following my heart resulted in caring too much for the approval of others, longing for relationships that didn't bring glory to God, and regularly struggling with jealousy and bitterness. Following my heart felt pretty hopeless.

Of course, my own inclination to follow my heart didn't begin with messages I picked up from songs on the radio or shows on TV. God's people have been following their hearts without the help of be-yourself branding for generations. Esau followed his heart in hunger and sold his birthright for a bowl of soup. Abraham followed the fear in his heart and lied to Abimelech. Joseph's brothers followed the envy in their hearts and sold Joseph into slavery. Moses followed his angry heart and murdered an Egyptian. King Saul followed his jealous heart into a downward spiral of murderous rage and depression. Peter followed his fearful heart and denied Jesus. Judas followed his heart's desire for money and power and delivered the Son of God into the hands of the enemy. Instead of the happy-clappy ending their hearts desired, they found sin, punishment, and death that could only be redeemed by the blood of Jesus.

Satan has been distorting God's plan for your emotions and the resulting feelings you experience from the very beginning. In the garden he tempted Eve to follow her heart by dangling her desire for wisdom right before her face. She responded by following her feelings headlong into disobedience—a decision which resulted in consequences you're still feeling today. And ever since, we've all been following suit. Your heart can't be trusted, and neither can mine. Author Jon Bloom explains:

> The "follow your heart" creed certainly isn't found in the Bible. The Bible actually thinks our hearts have a disease: "the heart is deceitful above all things, and desperately sick; who can understand it?" (Jer. 17:9). Jesus, the Great Physician, lists the grim symptoms of this disease: "out of the heart come evil thoughts, murder, adultery, sexual immorality, theft, false witness, slander" (Matt. 15:19). . . . The truth is that no one lies to us more than our own hearts. No one. They don't tell us the truth, they just tell us what we want. They are not benevolent, they are pathologically selfish. In fact, if we do what our hearts tell us to do we will pervert and impoverish every desire, every beauty, every person, every wonder, and every joy. Our hearts want to consume these things for our own self-glory and self-indulgence.[1]

I recognize that it may come as a shock that your heart can't be trusted. Maybe you've assumed that because you are "fearfully and wonderfully made" and your soul "knows it very well," your heart is therefore trustworthy (Ps. 139:14). But when you understand what Scripture says your heart is capable of—evil thoughts, murder, adultery, sexual immorality, theft, false witness, and slander—you'll also understand why it's not smart to follow it down the path of destruction. Paul writes to Timothy: "So flee youthful passions and pursue righteousness, faith, love, and peace along with those who call on the Lord from a pure heart" (2 Tim. 2:22). Growing in godliness requires you first and foremost to *stop following your heart.*

Follow God's Heart

Your emotions should lead you to fellowship with God, to understand and follow *his* heart. The psalmist writes, "But know that the LORD has set apart the godly for himself; the LORD hears when I call to him. Be angry, and do not sin; ponder in your own hearts on your beds, and be silent. Offer right sacrifices, and put your trust in the LORD" (Ps. 4:3–5). Your heart is not called to free expression, but to *holiness*. "For this is the will of God, your sanctification [or growth in godliness] . . . that each one of you know how to control his own body in holiness and honor, not in the passion of lust like the Gentiles who do not know God" (1 Thess. 4:3–5).

Instead of following your heart into sin, submit your feelings to the example of Jesus. Your High Priest is able to sympathize with your weakness. Because Jesus's heart has in every respect been tempted, and yet he remained without sin, he is your role model. Because he's familiar with your temptation, he offers you mercy, grace, and help in your greatest times of need (Heb. 4:15). Your feelings and emotions are an invitation to draw near to him. Instead of blindly following your feelings into foolish sin, take your heart to Jesus and ask him to help you obey.

Angry and bitter over a friend's betrayal? Take your anger to Jesus and ask him to help you pursue peace and desire forgiveness. Annoyed with your parents and tempted to disobey them? Go to Jesus and confess your hard heart; ask for grace to submit to authority even when your heart desires independence. Exhausted and feel like giving in to sin? Bring your feelings of weary surrender to God and ask for his strength to fight off temptation. Instead of following your heart, present your feelings as a living sacrifice, holy and acceptable to God (Rom. 12:1). Growing in godliness requires you to *follow God's heart*.

Obey When You're Not Feeling It

Following God's heart means obeying his commands—pursuing purity and holiness—even when you don't feel like it. God's laws and commands are like a compass, designed to point you to what's good and right. Consider the safety warning the Lord speaks to the Israelites in Deuteronomy 30:16–18:

> If you obey the commandments of the Lord your God that I command you today, by loving the Lord your God, by walking in his ways, and by keeping his commandments and his statutes and his rules, then you shall live and multiply, and the Lord your God will bless you in the land that you are entering to take possession of it. But if your heart turns away, and you will not hear, but are drawn away to worship other gods and serve them, I declare to you today that you shall surely perish.

Obeying God is equated with life and blessing, while disobeying is equated with death and curse. When you allow your feelings to overrule God's commands, you essentially choose to live as an enemy of Christ whose "end is destruction" (Phil. 3:18–19). *Growing in godliness means obeying God's commands even when you're not feeling it.*

You Are Not a Robot, You're a Steward

You may be wondering, "Are you saying that in order to be godly, I have to ignore my feelings?" No! I'm actually saying it's important to pay attention to your feelings because they play an important role in your growth in godliness! You are the handiwork of the God who feels. God loves (1 John 4:19), delights (Deut. 28:63), and is filled with the fullness of joy (Ps. 16:11). He is also righteously grieved (Gen. 6:6), jealous (Deut. 6:15), and angry (Deut. 31:17). God's emotions throughout Scripture help you to know his character and holiness. Similarly, your emotions expose both your own (often lacking) character and your own progress in holiness. While we aren't meant to follow our emotions, we should learn from them.

I'm not asking you to become an emotionless robot. Nor am I advising you to internally flip a switch and simply stop feeling all emotion. I am inviting you to *steward* your feelings and your emotional responses in a way that expresses obedience to God and the desire for holiness. This is faithful *emotional stewardship*. Stewardship simply means to manage or look after. In 1 Corinthians, Paul says Christians should be regarded as servants of Christ and stewards of the mysteries of God: "Moreover, it is required of stewards that they be found faithful" (1 Cor. 4:1–2). You faithfully steward your emotions when you submit your feelings and responses to Christ's lordship, instead of defaulting to act on your own feelings. Do your feelings and emotions most often point you toward God? Or do they lead you away from him? Do you regularly steward your emotions, or manage your feelings, in a way that points to God's faithfulness?

Job is a great example of faithful emotional stewardship. His life wasn't all roses, and his circumstances didn't set him up for a life overflowing with rainbows and sunshine. Instead, he faced severe trials and tribulation. Satan stripped him of his property, killed his children, and eventually took his health, but Job didn't follow his heart into sin. No doubt, Job felt despair, grief, sorrow, and loss. But Job trusted God and relied on his goodness rather than his feelings and circumstances. Through his feelings of intense grief, Job trusted the good character of God, obeyed his commands, and responded, "The LORD gave, and the LORD has taken away; blessed be the name of the LORD" (Job 1:21). Job remained confident in hope and convinced of God's goodness.

The Psalms are filled with even more examples of godly emotional stewardship. The psalmists were unafraid to confess their doubts, fears, and weakness of heart to God. They didn't stuff their feelings; they faithfully brought them before the Lord. "Be gracious to me, O LORD! See my affliction from those who hate me, O you who lift me up from the gates of death, that I may recount all your praises ... [and] rejoice in your salvation" (Ps. 9:13–14). The psalmists desired that their hearts be fully yielded to God, so they might readily bring him praise.

And most obviously, Jesus sets the gold standard of emotional stewardship. Hebrews 4:15 says, "We do not have a high priest who is unable to sympathize with our weaknesses, but one who in every respect has been tempted as we are, yet without sin." Jesus modeled righteous anger when he turned the tables over in the temple. He wept when Lazarus died. He rested when he felt weary. He corrected his disciples in love when he had every right to be frustrated with them. *Growing in godliness means stewarding your feelings to the glory of God, by following the example of Jesus.*

Live God's Truth

What do you do with your feelings? Do you let them control you? Or do you surrender them to God and ask for his help? Do you regularly see your feelings as an opportunity to throw your weight around and get what you want, or as a doorway to developing holiness? First Thessalonians 4:7–8 says, "For God has not called us for impurity, but in holiness. Therefore whoever disregards this, disregards not man but God, who gives his Holy Spirit to you." If your feelings control your choices, your actions, and your life, you are following your heart, obeying the culture's messages, and disregarding God's truth.

Instead of following your heart, ask God to help you actively follow his heart and the example of Jesus. Invite others into the process. When your feelings seem overwhelming, pray and confess this to God. Then, confess your struggles to a Christian that you trust. Ask her to help you think through challenging emotions and situations with biblical wisdom. Ask her to pray with you so that you might be strengthened by God's grace. Ask for regular outside input when you're not in the heat of an emotional crisis. Your parents and friends have a front-row seat to how you behave on a daily basis; they've likely observed your fluctuating emotions and could give you their perspective on how you tend to handle your feelings. They might be able to identify specific emotions like anger, fear, or disappointment, which tend to lead you into sin. Ask the people you trust to help hold you accountable in the way you steward your emotions. Be ready to humbly accept truthful feedback when they point out potential growth areas.

Your fickle feelings and untrustworthy heart need not control you. Your life and actions should demonstrate obedience to Christ. As a teenager who's likely experiencing the highs and lows of raging hormones and the resulting unpredictable emotions, the gospel frees you from being controlled by your feelings and gives you the hope of conforming to him. As you grow in godliness, ignore the worldly messages of "be who you want to be, live your truth, and follow your heart." And instead, strive to honor Christ in stewarding your emotions.

Grow Up by Stewarding Your Feelings

The mature Christian woman follows God's heart instead of her own and submits her feelings to the obedience of Christ.

Practice Stewarding Your Feelings

* *Ask* someone you live with to share her outside perspective on how you tend to express your emotions and feelings. Would she say that you follow your heart even when it's sinful? Or do you die to self in order to follow the heart of God? (These are hard questions that take humility to ask, but they are a quick way to begin to put sinful feelings to death.)

* *Identify* particular emotions that tend to be regular areas of temptation. Do you struggle most often with anger? Fear? Unbelief? Be specific about ways your emotions lead you into sinful action.

* *Write* Psalm 139:23 and read over (or memorize) it when you're facing the temptation to follow your feelings.

* *Pray* for God to use your emotions and your feelings to lead you to him. Ask him to give you a heart that's sensitive to his commands, quick to repentance, and holds fast to obedience. Confess your need for his intervention and help.

10

Examine Your Fruit

In 2013 a group of five ninth-grade girls in Denmark noticed a peculiar coincidence. On the nights they plugged their cell phones in to charge next to their beds, they seemed to be more distracted at school the following day. This observation prompted the girls to wonder what other consequences their cell phones might cause. The girls decided to test their theory with a school science project.[1] Could cell phone radiation really be to blame for their lack of concentration? Should they change the ways they charged and used them? The teenagers didn't have the time, experience, or funding to fully test their theory on human brains, so they settled on examining the effects of cell phone radiation on plants.

In two rooms, the girls placed six trays of *lepidium sativum*, a fast-growing herb also known as garden cress. In one room, they placed two internet routers designed to emit roughly the same amount of radiation as ordinary cell phones. In the second room, the garden cress remained radiation-free. Over the next twelve days, they watched, measured, and snapped pictures documenting each notable result. By the end of their experiment, the girls' seed trays looked markedly different from one another. Despite the fact that the seeds are known to be easy to grow and tolerant of any climate, the ones left next to the routers hadn't grown at all. Meanwhile, the radiation-free plants next door continued to thrive and grow.

The girls' experiment garnered top honors in a regional science competition, the interest of a Swedish neuroscience professor, and worldwide attention from news outlets and the science community at large. If radiation from a router could inhibit the growth of a plant, what did this mean for the human brain? What could these two trays of seeds—one green and healthy and the other failing to thrive—teach the world? Could their findings help protect a generation of growing tech-lovers? I suppose we will have to wait and see.

Examine Your Growth

What do Wi-Fi signals and garden cress seeds have to do with your growth in godliness? Both use *life* and *growth* as the measure by which they evaluate health. Both see failure to grow as an indicator of trouble.

In the Denmark girls' experiment, an outside source prevented the growth of those garden cress seeds, even though they couldn't make any conclusive determinations. Unlike our Denmark friends' science project, your spiritual life doesn't need to suffer from the failure to draw conclusions. Jesus explains the source of your growth in John 15:4–5:

> Abide in me, and I in you. As the branch cannot bear fruit by itself, unless it abides in the vine, neither can you, unless you abide in me. I am the vine; you are the branches. Whoever

abides in me and I in him, he it is that bears much fruit, for apart from me you can do nothing.

If you aren't growing in godliness, this is a sign of trouble. At the root of failure to grow in godliness is always the spiritual problem of failure to live in Christ. If you want to grow, you'll need what Martin Luther referred to as *fides viva*—living faith. Pastor R. C. Sproul expands on this living faith:

> It is a faith that immediately brings forth the fruits of repentance and righteousness. If we say we have faith, but no works follow, that is clear evidence that our faith is not genuine. True faith always produces real conformity to Christ. If justification happens to us, the sanctification surely will follow. If there is no sanctification, it means that there never was any justification.[2]

Growth always occurs in the lives of those who have been granted new life in the name of Jesus. If you have the desire to know God and the longing to be more like Christ, you can thank God for planting the seed of faith in your heart (Mark 4:14), keeping it safely in the good soil, and growing and producing fruit. And while only God can give the growth (1 Cor. 3:7), you have a part in the process! You are called to partner with him by responding in faith. Mark 4:20 says the seeds "that were sown on the good soil are the ones who hear the word and accept it and bear fruit, thirtyfold and sixtyfold and a hundredfold."

In the life of a Christian, *fruit* is the sign of life, a demonstration of the Spirit's work-in-progress. As you grow in godliness, your life will be increasingly filled with the fruit of the Spirit. "Love, joy, peace, patience, kindness, goodness, faithfulness, gentleness, self-control" will all be yours (Gal. 5:22–23). If you have faith even the size of the smallest mustard seed, when it is sown in the good soil, it will certainly grow up "and become larger than all the garden plants and put out large branches" (Mark 4:32). The increasing "fruit of righteousness" (Phil. 1:11) that comes through Jesus Christ will be a noticeable change, and God will use the fruit in your life to serve others with the gospel, changing lives and multiplying his kingdom (Col. 1:5–6).

Examine your life. Is there fruit? How would you describe your growth in godliness? Are your seeds of faith dead as a doornail, like the Wi-Fi-poisoned *lepidium sativum*? Or is your faith *fides viva*, a living faith—growing up and increasingly yielding more and more fruit every day?

Train for Growth

As a child, I planted an apple tree in my backyard. I crunched into a juicy apple's flesh at lunch, immediately headed out back, dug a hole in the ground, tossed a seed in, watered it, and then waited for it to grow. Each day I'd check for signs of growth. As the tiny twigs of new life began to sprout from the ground, I imagined the forthcoming apple feast ahead: my own stash of apples, fresh-squeezed apple juice, apple pie à la mode—you get the idea. Imagine my disappointment when the growth never came. That stupid stick stayed a stupid stick. No apples, no juice, no pie. Where did I go wrong?

I failed to train myself in the ways of apple growing. I had no clue that growing an apple tree involved so much time and effort. Apple trees aren't self-pollinating, so they need to be planted in pairs. I didn't know that, so of course I planted only one seed. They also take eight to ten years to produce fruit! That's a lot of waiting by the window. Training would really have helped. No training = no apple pie.

In the New Testament, Paul celebrates the spiritual fruit produced when believers grow in godliness. In 2 Thessalonians 1:3 he gives thanks to God because the Thessalonians' faith was "growing abundantly," and their love for one another was increasing. While we know God gives the growth, and true believers abiding in Christ will grow, there is value in cultivating growth. At the close of his second letter, Peter encourages his beloved brothers and sisters in Christ to put forth their own effort to "grow in the grace and knowledge of our Lord and Savior Jesus Christ" (2 Pet. 3:18). You have a part in the growth process! The fruit of righteousness comes through Jesus Christ (Phil. 1:11) who trains you (Heb. 12:11) for his glory.

> For the grace of God has appeared, bringing salvation for all people, *training us* to renounce ungodliness and worldly passions, and to live self-controlled, upright, and godly lives in the present age, waiting for our blessed hope, the appearing of the glory of our great God and Savior Jesus Christ, who gave himself for us to redeem us from all lawlessness and to purify for himself a people for his own possession who are zealous for good works. (Titus 2:11–14)

Train yourself for godliness (1 Tim. 4:7–8). It is of value in every way and holds promise for the present life and also for the life to come.

Examine Your Fruit

Growing in godliness takes a lifetime. As you grow, you will be tempted to grow weary, to lose sight of the goal of godliness, and to wonder if God is really at work in your life at all. Theologian John Owen said the growth of trees and plants takes place so slowly that it is not easily seen. You may notice little daily change. But, over time, you will see that a great change has taken place. "So it is with grace. Sanctification is a progressive, lifelong work

(Prov. 4:18). It is an amazing work of God's grace and it is a work to be prayed for (Rom. 8:27)."[3]

Do you long to grow in godliness? Do you pray for maturity in Christ? Are you training yourself in righteousness so your life might be characterized by "the holiness without which no one will see the Lord" (Heb. 12:14)? Examine the fruit of your growth. And where you find death, pray for new life. Where you find immaturity, pray for maturity. It is my prayer that if you aren't striving to grow in godliness, you would begin today. And if you are, that you'll stay the course toward maturity in Christ.

When you die to yourself and come alive in Christ, you live to glorify God by growing in godliness. In the process, your life bursts forth with the fruits of Christian maturity. Your growth in godliness isn't for your own posterity. It's not to impress your parents, your friends, or your youth group. As you grow to look more like Jesus, you will more clearly display God's likeness to the watching world. God will use the fruits of righteousness in your life to plant seeds of faith in the lives of others. And in doing so, Christ builds his kingdom. This ever-increasing, always growing, fruitful maturity in Christ is the ultimate way your life can bring glory to God. Never stop growing. Wait patiently as your *fides viva*—living faith—grows:

> Until we all attain to the unity of the faith and of the knowledge of the Son of God, to mature [wo]manhood, to the measure of the stature of the fullness of Christ, so that we may no longer be children, tossed to and fro by the waves and carried about by every wind of doctrine, by human cunning, by craftiness in deceitful schemes. Rather, speaking the truth in love, we are to *grow up in every way* into him who is the head, into Christ, from whom the whole body, joined and held together by every joint with which it is equipped, when each part is

working properly, makes the body grow so that it builds itself up in love. (Eph. 4:13–16)

God wants to use every area of your life—each experience, challenge, and privilege—as spiritual fertilizer, feeding your growth in godliness. How does God intend for you to grow? By calling you to the process of sanctification. By teaching you to work to bring him glory. By demonstrating his sovereign goodness. By helping you address your limitations. By providing his word, building his church, and through the fellowship of prayer. And in the process, your words, emotions, and the existence of the fruits of the spirit will all serve as signs of your spiritual health and life.

Strive to *grow*. Martin Luther wrote, "This life, therefore, is not godliness, but the process of becoming godly, not health but getting well, not being but becoming, not rest but exercise. We are not now what we shall be, but we are on the way. The process is not yet finished, but it is actively going on. This is not the goal, but it is the right road. At present everything does not gleam and sparkle, but everything is being cleansed."[4] Beloved, grow in the grace and knowledge of Jesus Christ (2 Pet. 3:18) and you will most certainly *grow in godliness*.

Grow Up by Examining Your Fruit

The mature Christian woman abides in Christ and bears increasing spiritual fruit.

Practice Examining Your Fruit

✱ *Ask* your parents or a Christian mentor to make a list of several ways they've observed your growth in godliness over time. Ask them to help you identify a few areas you could commit to growing in godliness in over the next year.

✱ *Identify* a few practical ways that you could strive for godliness in these potential growth areas you just listed in the question above. How could you practice them in your home? At school? In your local church?

✱ *Write* John 15:4–6 on a date of your choosing on your calendar. Whether it's in a month, three months, or a year, use this date as an opportunity to revisit the ways you've seen God's grace actively growing you in godliness. Reflect on how abiding in Christ has resulted in growth. Write down your observations in a journal and determine if you'd like to continue focusing on these areas of growth or commit to pursuing growth in additional areas. Commit to your next date of evaluation.

✱ *Pray* Ephesians 4:13–16 over your life, asking that God would help you "attain to the unity of the faith and of the knowledge of the Son of God to mature [woman]hood, to the measure of the stature of the fullness of Christ," so that you may no longer be tossed by the waves and "carried about by every wind of doctrine, by human cunning, by craftiness in deceitful schemes." Ask God to help you *"grow up in every way* into him who is the head, into Christ, from whom the whole body, joined and held together by every joint with which it is equipped, when each part is working properly, makes the body grow so that it builds itself up in love."

Acknowledgments

One Puritan prayer pleads, "May I live by thee, live for thee, never be satisfied with my Christian progress but as I resemble Christ; And may my conformity to his principles, temper, and conduct grow hourly in my life."[1] To all those who have modeled this desire with their lives and challenged me to grow in godliness, you've exercised excruciating patience with me and I am eternally grateful.

Thank you to my husband, Kyle, who loves me as Christ loved the church and lives with me in the most understanding ways imaginable. You help me see and savor Jesus more clearly, and I delight to work in ministry by your side. Even though it perplexes me that I am publishing a book and not my darling Captain English, you are still my favorite theologian and editor. Thank you for ensuring I feel encouraged to write and have the time and brain space to do so. Thank you to my children—Madeline, Collin, Jude, Spencer, and Rex—for your patience as I've locked my door to write and for your excitement in seeing this book become "a *real* book!"

Thank you to my long-haul friends for sticking with me through many, many years of awkward growth in godliness. You have been tangible demonstrations of Christ's love, unconditional forgiveness, and selfless grace in my life. Allisa Hovis, with you, friendship is not duty but delight. From Houston to Baltimore, your gentle wisdom, generosity, and self-control regularly sharpen me, and your texts, stories, and cat videos are good for my soul. Julia Nutter, your loyal friendship and steady voice of reason appeared at a providential moment in my life, and it is God's mercy that he moved your family beside us in Maryland. Through sorrows and trials, I am thankful we are learning more of God's faithfulness together.

Thank you to Collin Hansen for casting a vision for more women writers in the early years of TGC. You, Gloria Furman, and Matt Smethurst have each shaped me into a better writer. Thank you to Gloria, Jen Wilkin, and Melissa Kruger for lovingly cheering me on over the years, all the while pouring in measureless wisdom and encouragement. Thank you to Megan Hill, whose friendship in this writing world has served to both strengthen my writing muscles and encourage my weary heart. Thanks for always shooting straight, making me laugh, and explaining the *Chicago Manual of Style* while you're on vacation. Thank you to Dave DeWit and the team at Crossway for taking a chance on me. Your grace and kindness in this process has only strengthened my respect and love for Crossway. I'm grateful to be a part of the family.

And last but not least, thank you to my church family, Imprint Community Church. Your partnership in the gospel, your commitment to our fellowship, your growing love for Jesus, and the way you energetically serve our community is a constant encouragement. You are the tangible hands and feet of Christ in my everyday life, and I am grateful to labor together for growth in godliness and Christ's kingdom.

To God be the glory!

Notes

Chapter 1: Live to Grow

1. Wayne Grudem, *Systematic Theology: An Introduction to Biblical Doctrine* (Grand Rapids, MI: Zondervan, 1994), 74.
2. Jerry Bridges, *The Practice of Godliness* (Colorado Springs, CO: Navpress, 1983), 20.
3. Bridges, *The Practice of Godliness*, 18.

Chapter 3: Relax and Trust Him

1. Jerry Bridges, *Trusting God* (Colorado Springs, CO: NavPress, 1988), 29.

Chapter 4: Learn from Your Limits

1. Jen Wilkin, *None Like Him: 10 Ways God Is Different from Us (and Why That's a Good Thing)* (Wheaton, IL: Crossway, 2016), 25.

Chapter 5: Search for Riches

1. "Larry Page," *Forbes* online, last modified October 8, 2018, https://www.forbes.com/profile/larry-page/.
2. Jillian D'Onfro, "The Spectacular Life of Google Founder and Alphabet CEO Larry Page," *Business Insider* online, March 17, 2016, https://www.businessinsider.com/the-life-career-of-larry-page-2016-3/.
3. "Top 10 Findings on Teens and the Bible," Barna, August 26, 2016, https://www.barna.com/research/top-10-findings-teens-bible/.
4. "Top 10 Findings on Teens and the Bible," Barna.
5. John Piper, "He Will Send His Angel Before You," sermon, Bethlehem Baptist Church, Minneapolis, August 8, 1982, https://www.desiringgod.org/messages/he-will-send-his-angel-before-you/.
6. Piper, "He Will Send His Angel Before You."

Chapter 6: Love His Church

1. "Atheism Doubles among Generation Z," Barna, January 24, 2018, https://www.barna.com/research/atheism-doubles-among-generation-z/.

2. "Gen Z: Your Questions Answered," Barna, February 6, 2018, https://www.barna.com/research/gen-z-questions-answered/.

3. John Piper, "I Will Not Leave Jesus—But I'm Done with the Church," December 16, 2015, in *Ask Pastor John*, interview, https://www.desiringgod.org/interviews/i-will-not-leave-jesus-but-i-m-done-with-the-church.

4. R. C. Sproul, "What Is the Church?" *Tabletalk Magazine*, July 1, 2016, https://www.ligonier.org/learn/articles/what-church/.

5. Brett McCracken, *Uncomfortable: The Awkward and Essential Challenge of Christian Community* (Wheaton, IL: Crossway, 2017), 38–39.

Chapter 8: Use Your Words

1. Christin Ditchfield, *A Way with Words: What Women Should Know about the Power They Possess* (Wheaton, IL: Crossway, 2010), 56–57.

Chapter 9: Steward Your Feelings

1. Jon Bloom, "Don't Follow Your Heart (New Book)," Desiring God website, November 18, 2015, https://www.desiringgod.org/articles/dont-follow-your-heart-new-book.

Chapter 10: Examine Your Fruit

1. Daniel Bean, "Can WiFi Signals Stunt Plant Growth?," *ABC News* online, May 24, 2013, https://abcnews.go.com/Technology/can-wifi-signals-stunt-plant-growth/blogEntry?id=19251950/.

2. R. C. Sproul, *The Holiness of God* (Sanford, FL: Ligonier Ministries, 2010), 202.

3. John Owen, *The Holy Spirit* (Carlisle, PA: Banner of Truth, 1965), 108–9.

4. Martin Luther, *Career of the Reformer II*, eds. Helmut T. Lehmann and George W. Forell, vol. 32 of *Luther's Works*, American Edition, eds. Jaroslav Pelikan and Helmut T. Lehmann (Philadelphia: Muhlenberg Press, 1958), 24.

Acknowledgments

1. Arthur Bennett, ed., *The Valley of Vision: A Collection of Puritan Prayers and Devotions* (Carlisle, PA: Banner of Truth, 1975), 115.

Scripture Index